Life in the Caribbean

Keith Thompson, editor

©Wikipedia 2010
Life in the Caribbean
Keith Thompson, editor

ISBN 978-9987-16-015-0

New Africa Press
Dar es Salaam, Tanzania

Contents

Acknowledgements

**Chapter One:
Anguilla**

**Chapter Two:
Antigua and Barbuda**

**Chapter Three:
The Bahamas**

**Chapter Four:
Barbados**

**Chapter Five:
British Virgin Islands**

**Chapter Six:
Cayman Islands**

**Chapter Seven:
Dominica**

**Chapter Eight:
Grenada**

**Chapter Nine:
Jamaica**

Acknowledgements

THIS work is a compilation of some material from Wikipedia. It's published under the terms of the Wikipedia licence which allows the use of such material by members of the general public for commercial and noncommercial purposes.

While many people can get the material from Wikipedia, compilation of the articles in a single volume enables readers to have easy access to the information about the Caribbean islands covered in this work.

The articles have been modified in many parts. Some parts have been left out. Other parts have been re-written, sometimes adding new material, in order to provide an organised and readable work on the Caribbean islands.

In fact, a substantial portion of the material in every chapter has been re-written.

Apart from re-writing the material, I have also provided additional information. I am the primary source of some of the material I have added to this work. The information is derived from my own personal experience.

And in some cases, my own knowledge of some of the subjects has also been incorporated into this study.

Therefore what you're going to read in this volume and in subsequent works on the Caribbean islands under my name is not entirely a reproduction of Wikipedia articles, although it is in many cases. There is new material interspersed throughout the book here and there. But the new material does not constitute the bulk of this work.

The fact that many parts of the Wikipedia articles have been re-rewritten does not mean that the content has been changed substantially. It's essentially the same.

The focus is on the English-speaking islands in the Caribbean.

Chapter One:

Anguilla

ANGUILLA is a British overseas territory in the Caribbean. It is the most northerly of the Leeward Islands in the Lesser Antilles.

It consists of the main island of Anguilla itself, approximately 16 miles long by 3.1 miles wide at its widest point, together with a number of much smaller islands and cays with no permanent population.

The island's capital is The Valley.

Anguilla has an area of 35 square miles. It had a population of 13,500 in 2006.

History

Anguilla was first settled by Amerindian tribes who migrated from South America. The earliest Amerindian artifacts found on Anguilla have been dated to around 1300 BC, and remains of settlements date from 600 AD. The date of European discovery is uncertain. Some sources claim that Columbus sighted the island in 1493, while others state that the island was first discovered by the French in 1564 or 1565.

The name Anguilla is derived from the word for "eel" in any of the various Romance languages – modern Spanish: *anguila*; French: *anguille*; Italian: *anguilla* – and was probably chosen because the island is shaped like an eel.

Anguilla was first colonised by English settlers from Saint Kitts. They first moved to Anguilla in 1650.

The French temporarily took over the island in 1666. But under the Treaty of Breda, the island was returned to the English in 1667.

Other early arrivals included Europeans from Antigua and Barbados. It is likely that some of these early Europeans brought enslaved Africans with them. Historians confirm that African slaves lived in the region in the early seventeenth century. For example, Africans from Senegal lived in St. Christopher (today St. Kitts) in 1626. By 1672 a slave depot existed on the island of Nevis, serving the Leeward Islands.

While the time of the arrival of Africans in Anguilla is difficult to determine, archival evidence indicates a substantial presence of at least 100 of them on the island by 1683.

In 1967 Britain granted Saint Kitts and Nevis full internal autonomy.

Anguilla was also incorporated into the unified dependency with Saint Kitts and Nevis. This led to two rebellions in 1967 and 1969 – Anguillian Revolution – headed by Ronald Webster, and a brief period of the island's self-declared independence from the Saint Kitts and Nevis dependency.

British authority was fully restored in July 1971. In

1980, Anguilla was finally allowed to secede and become a separate British dependency, now officially known as a British overseas territory.

Politics

Anguilla is a multi-party democracy governed as a British dependency under a parliamentary system. The chief minister is the head of government.

Executive power is exercised by the government. Legislative power is vested in both the government and the House of Assembly. And the Judiciary is independent of the executive and the legislature.

The law of Anguilla is a combination of common law and statute and is heavily based on English law.

The United Nations Committee on Decolonisation includes Anguilla on the United Nations list of Non-Self-Governing Territories.

Military

The United Kingdom is responsible for the island's defence. But there are no active garrisons or armed forces on the island.

Geography

Anguilla is one of the Leeward Islands which lie between the Caribbean Sea in the west and the open Atlantic Ocean in the east.

It's a long, flat, dry, scrub-covered coral island south and east of Puerto Rico and north of the Windward chain. Located north of Saint Martin, it's separated from that island by the Anguilla Channel.

It has no significant elevations and its terrain consists entirely of beaches, dunes and low limestone bluffs. The soil is generally thin and poor, supporting only scrub vegetation.

Anguilla is noted for its spectacular and ecologically important coral reefs. Apart from the main island of Anguilla itself, the territory includes a number of other smaller islands and cays. Most of them are very small and uninhabited.

Anguilla's highest elevation, Crocus Hill, is 213 feet. It's among the cliffs that line the northern shore.

The numerous bays – Barnes, Little, Rendezvous, Shoal, and Road – lure many vacationers to this tropical island. The coast and the beautiful, pristine beaches are integral to the tourism-based economy of Anguilla. Because of island's warm climate, the beaches can be used year-round.

Climate

Northeastern trade winds keep this tropical island cool and dry. Average annual temperature is 80.6°F. July–October is its hottest period; December–February, its coolest.

The island is subject to both sudden tropical storms and hurricanes which occur from July to October. It suffered damage from Hurricane Luis in 1995.

Economy

Anguilla's thin arid soil is largely unsuitable for agriculture, and the island has few land-based natural resources. Its main industries are tourism, offshore incorporation and management, offshore banking, and fishing. Many foreign-owned insurance and financial businesses are based in Anguilla.

The economy also depends heavily on remittances of Anguillans who live in other countries, especially in North

America and Britain.

The economy, and especially the tourism sector, suffered a setback due to the effects of Hurricane Luis which hit the island territory in September 1995 but recovered in 1996. Hotels were hit particularly hard during that time. Another economic setback occurred during the aftermath of Hurricane Lenny in 2000.

Increased activity in the tourism industry, which has spurred the growth of the construction sector, has contributed to economic growth.

Anguillan officials have also put substantial effort into developing the offshore financial sector, which is small, but growing. A comprehensive package of financial services legislation was enacted in late 1994. In the medium term, prospects for the economy will depend largely on the tourism sector and, therefore, on revived income growth in the industrialized nations as well as on favourable weather conditions.

The economy of Anguilla is expanding rapidly, especially the tourism sector which is driving major new developments in partnerships with multi-national companies. This boom, beginning gently during 2005-2006, accelerated through 2007 and is expected to continue for years.

Anguilla's currency is the East Caribbean dollar, though the US dollar is also widely accepted. The exchange rate is fixed to the US dollar at US$1 = EC $2.68.

Transport

Transport is simpler than in many countries mainly because of the island's small size.. There is no public transport such as bus and rail systems because there aren't enough people to justify the establishment of such an infrastructure. However, Anguilla's roads are better maintained than the transport networks on many of the other Caribbean islands.

Cars are the main means of transport, with driving on the left-hand side of the road as in the United Kingdom. Although speed limits rarely exceed 30 miles per hour and traffic moves slowly, it doesn't take long to get anywhere because of the the island's small size.

Taxi service is has set rates which are published in tourist guides. In addition to regular transport, taxis often offer island tours lasting several hours. Fares must be paid in cash.

Ferries offer transport from Anguilla to other islands. The ferry from Blowing Point to Marigot in St. Martin, known to the locals as the Haddad Express, runs all day into the night time every 20 minutes to half an hour. With no reservations required, taking the ferry is simple and inexpensive. Ferries can also be chartered to other destinations.

Other means of transport include bikes, mopeds, motorcycles and walking. Because of the territory's small size and flatter terrain, these methods make more sense on Anguilla than on many other Caribbean islands.

Cars, bikes, mopeds and motorcycles are can be rented at reasonable prices. Both well-known car rental agencies and local companies operate rental businesses. Groups may also charter a private bus for excursions.

Anguilla is served by Wallblake Airport. The primary runway can accommodate moderate-sized aircraft. Services connect to various other Caribbean islands but the airport cannot receive large jets. And there are no direct flights to or from continental America or Europe.

Aside from taxis, there is no public transport on the island.

Demographics

The vast majority of the people (90.08%) are black, descendants of slaves from Africa. Growing minorities include whites (3.74%) and people of mixed race (4.65%), according to 2001 census figures.

About 72% of the population is Anguillian and 28% non-Anguillian (2001 census). Of the non-Anguillian population, many are citizens of the United States, United Kingdom, St Kitts & Nevis, the Dominican Republic, Jamaica and Nigeria.

The years 2006 and 2007 saw an influx of large numbers of Chinese, Indian, and Mexican workers, brought in as labour for major tourist developments due to the local population not being large enough to support the labour requirements.

Culture

The Anguilla National Trust (ANT) was established in 1988 and opened its offices in 1993 charged with the responsibility of preserving the heritage of the island, including its cultural heritage. The Trust has programmes encouraging Anguillian writers and the preservation of the island's history.

The island's cultural history begins with the Taino Indians. Artifacts have been found around the island, telling of life before European settlers arrived.

As throughout the Caribbean, holidays are a cultural fixture. Anguilla's most important holidays are of historic as much as cultural importance – particularly the anniversary of the emancipation (previously August Monday in the Park), celebrated as the Summer Festival. British holidays, such as the Queen's birthday, are also celebrated.

Religion

According to the 2001 census Christianity is Anguilla's predominant religion, with 29 percent of the population practising Anglicanism. Another 23.9 percent are Methodist.

Other churches on the island include Seventh-day Adventist, Baptist, Roman Catholic, and Jehovah's Witnesses.

Between 1992 and 2001 the number of followers of the Church of God and Pentecostal churches increased considerably.

There are at least fifteen churches on the island, several of architectural interest.

Although a minority on the island, it is an important location to followers of Rastafarian religion. Anguilla is the birthplace of Robert Athlyi Rogers, author of *The Holy Piby* which has had a strong influence on Rastafarian beliefs.

Various other religions are practised as well.

Language

Today most of the people in Anguilla speak a British-influenced variety of Standard English.

Other languages are also spoken on the island, including varieties of Spanish, Chinese and the languages of other immigrants.

However, the most common language other than Standard English is the island's own English-lexifier Creole language (not to be confused with French Creole spoken in islands such as Haiti, Martinique, and Guadeloupe).

It is referred to locally by terms such as "dialect" (pronounced "dialec"), or "Anguillian." It has its main roots in early varieties of English and West African languages and is similar to the dialects spoken in English-speaking islands throughout the Eastern Caribbean.

Anguillan Creole is similar to varieties of Virgin Islands Creole. The number of speakers of Anguillan Creole is less than 10,000. Anguillan Creole does not have the status of an official language.

Music of Anguilla

The music of Anguilla is part of the Lesser Antillean music. It's a product of cultural fusion rooted in the diverse cultural origins of the people who have inhabited the territory through the centuries.

The earliest people of the island were the Caribs and Arawaks who arrived from South America. English settlers from St. Kitts and the Irish later colonised the island. But unlike in other Caribbean islands, the plantation system of agriculture that relied on chattel slavery never took root in Anguilla, causing a distinctly independent cultural makeup.

The most recent influences on Anguilla's musical life come from elsewhere in the Caribbean, especially the music of Trinidad and Tobago, and Jamaica. Other musical influences have come from abroad, especially the United States and the United Kingdom.

Anguilla's Rastafarian heritage has also played a major role in the island's music and culture and has produced influential figures such as activist Ijahnya Christian and Robert Athlyi Rogers, author of *The Holy Piby*.

The island has produced a number of popular reggae, calypso, soca and country musicians. Of all these, the last form of music is unique in the Anguillian and Caribbean cultural and musical context. Country music is not an integral part of Caribbean popular music.

Anguilla's Island Harbour, a village that once was an

Irish settlement on the east side of the island, is a major centre for local country music.

Soca is a major recent import that has become the most popular form of dance music on Anguilla. It's often accompanied by frenzied, sexualised dancing called *wukin up*.

Perhaps the most famous musician from Anguilla is Bankie Banx. He has recorded more than ten albums and has played with music legends such as Bob Dylan, Jimmy Cliff, and Jimmy Buffett.

He has also opened a popular music bar called the Dune Preserve, built in order to save the Rendezvous Bay dune. The Dune Preserve is home to the Moonsplash Annual Music Festival.

More recent popular successes include the soca group, Xtreme Band, which gained regional fame after its success in the 2001 Carnival.

Music institutions in Anguilla include the Soroptimist Club and the annual Tranquility Jazz Festival, though the island's most famous music celebration is Carnival, held near the beginning of August (the first Friday after the first Monday). The Carnival celebration includes calypso competitions, *j'ouvert*, street dances, boat races, costumed parades and stilt walking, and beach-side barbecues.

Anguillans also celebrate the anniversary of emancipation in August, and British holidays like the Queen's birthday.

For the first time in 2005, Anguilla was home to a country music festival which was promoted by American country star Billy Ray Cyrus and other American musicians.

Other popular musicians from Anguilla include Evan Webster, the most famous recent performer to emerge from the island's country music scene.

Sports

Boat racing has deep roots in Anguillian culture/ It's the national sport.

There are regular sailing regattas on national holidays such as Carnival which are contested by locally built and designed boats. A regatta is a term (Latin for 'boat') used to describe either a boat race or or series of boat races.

The boats have names and have sponsors who print their logo on the sails.

As in many other former British colonies, cricket is also a popular sport.

Anguilla is the home of Omari Banks who played for the West Indies Cricket Team. Another Anguillian, Cardigan Connor, played first-class cricket for English countryside Hampshire and was *chef de mission* (team manager) for Anguilla's Commonwealth Games team in 2002.

The Rugby Union is represented in Anguilla by the Anguilla Eels RFC formed in April 2006.

Chapter Two:

Antigua and Barbuda

ANTIGUA AND BARBUDA is a twin-island nation lying between the Caribbean Sea and the Atlantic Ocean.

It consists of two major inhabited islands, Antigua and Barbuda, and a number of smaller islands. Smaller islands include Great Bird, Green, Guinea, Long, Maiden and York Islands/

Separated by a few sea miles, the group of the islands which collectively constitute the island nation of Antigua and Barbuda is in the middle of the Leeward Islands which are part of the Lesser Antilles.

History

Antigua was first settled by Amerindians. Carbon-dating has established that the earliest settlements started around 3100 BCE. They were succeeded by the Ceramic Age pre-Columbian Arawak-speaking Saladoid people who migrated from the lower Orinoco River.

The Arawaks introduced agriculture. The grew the famous Antigua black pineapple, maize, sweet potatoes, chiles, guava, tobacco and cotton.

The indigenous West Indians made excellent sea-going vessels which they used to sail the Atlantic and the Caribbean. As a result, Caribs and Arawaks were able to colonise much of South America and the Caribbean islands. Their descendants still live in the region, especially in Brazil, Venezuela and Colombia.

Most Arawaks left Antigua around 1100 CE. Those who remained were later raided by the Caribs. According to the *Catholic Encyclopedia*, the Caribs' superior weapons and seafaring prowess allowed them to defeat most of the West Indian Arawak nations, enslaving some and possibly eating others.

The *Catholic Encyclopedia* does make it clear that the European invaders had some difficulty differentiating between the native peoples they encountered. As a result, the number and types of ethnic/tribal groups in existence at that time may have been much more varied and numerous than just the Carib and the Arawak.

According to *A Brief History of the Caribbean* (Jan Rogozinski, Penguin Putnam, Inc., September 2000), European and African diseases, malnutrition and slavery eventually killed most of the Caribbean's native population. But no researcher has conclusively proven any of these causes as the real reason for these deaths.

In fact, some historians believe that the psychological stress of slavery may also have played a part in the massive number of deaths amongst enslaved natives. Others believe that the reportedly abundant, but starchy, low-protein diet may have contributed to severe malnutrition of the Amerindians who were used to a diet fortified with protein from the sea.

The island of Antigua, originally called "Wa'ladli" by Arawaks, is today called the "Land of Wadadli" by locals. And it's possible Caribs called it "Wa'omoni."

Christopher Columbus may have named it "Santa Maria la Antigua" in 1493 after an icon in the Spanish Seville Cathedral.

But the Spaniards did not colonise Antigua because it lacked fresh water. It also had Caribs who were known for their ferocity.

The English settled on Antigua in 1632; Sir Christopher Codrington settled on Barbuda in 1684. And slavery which was introduced in 1684 to provide sugar plantations with abundant labour was abolished in 1834.

The British ruled Antigua and Barbuda from 1632 to 1981, with a brief French interlude in 1666.

The islands became an independent nation within the Commonwealth of Nations on 1 November 1981. Queen Elizabeth II became head of state. And Vere Cornwall Bird became the first prime minister.

Politics

Antigua and Barbuda has a parliamentary system. It's also a federal state. The governor-general represents the Queen.

Executive power is exercised by the government. And legislative power is vested in the government and the two chambers of parliament. The bicameral parliament consists of the senate and the house of representatives.

Since 1949, the multi-party system had been dominated by the populist Antigua Labour Party. However, the legislative election in 2004 saw the defeat of the longest-serving elected government in the Caribbean.

The island nation's judicial branch is the Eastern Caribbean Supreme Court which is based in Saint Lucia. Antigua is also a member of the Caribbean Court of

Justice.

The Supreme Court of Appeal was the British Judicial Committee of the Privy Council until 2001 when the nations of the Caribbean Community voted to abolish the right of appeal to the Privy Council in favour of a Caribbean Court of Justice.

Some debate between member countries repeatedly delayed the court's date of inauguration. And as of March 2005, only Barbados was set to replace appeals to the Privy Council with appeals the Caribbean Court of Justice which by then had become operational.

Geography

The island nation of Antigua and Barbuda lies in the eastern arc of the Leeward Islands of the Lesser Antilles which are located between the Atlantic Ocean and the Caribbean Sea.

Antigua is about 404 miles southeast of Puerto Rico. Barbuda is 30 miles north of Antigua. And the uninhabited island of Redonda is about 35 miles southwest of Antigua.

The largest island is Antigua. It's about 14 miles wide and 11 miles long covering an area of 108 square miles.

Barbuda has an area of 62 square miles., and Redonda only about one square mile.

The capital of Antigua and Barbuda is St. John's. It's located at St. John's Harbour on the northwestern coast of Antigua.

The main urban centre of Barbuda is Codrington located on Codrington Lagoon.

Mountains and hills

Antigua and Barbuda are low-lying islands whose terrain has been influenced more by limestone formations than volcanic activity.

The highest point on Antigua is Mount Obama, named after United States president, Barack Obama, who was elected in 2008. It was formerly known as Boggy Peak. It's 1309 feet high and is a remnant of a volcanic crater. It's located amid a bulge of hills of volcanic origin in the southwestern part of the island.

Barbuda's highest elevation is 146 feet and is part of the highland plateau east of Codrington.

The shorelines of both islands are greatly indented, with beaches, lagoons, and natural harbours. The islands are rimmed by reefs and shoals.

The islands have few streams and only a little rainfall. Both islands lack adequate amounts of fresh groundwater.

Redonda has no significant elevation.

Oceans and seas

Antigua and Barbuda are located in the eastern Caribbean Sea. The open Atlantic Ocean lies to the north and east. There are many coral reefs near the two main islands. The island of Guadeloupe lies to the south, on the far side of the Guadeloupe Passage from Antigua.

The coast and beaches

Antigua and Barbuda is famous for its beaches, especially those on Antigua. The most prominent feature of Barbuda's coastline is the natural lagoon on the western side of the island.

Climate

Wind

The islands' tropical climate is moderated by fairly constant northeast trade winds, with velocities ranging between 19 and 30 miles per hour. There is little precipitation because of the islands' low elevations.

Rainfall and temperature

Rainfall averages 39 inches per year. But the amount varies widely from season to season. The wettest period is between September and November.

The islands generally experience low humidity and recurrent droughts. Hurricanes strike on an average of once a year.

Temperatures average 80.6°F, ranging from 73.4°F in the winter to 86°F in the summer and autumn. The coolest period is between December and February.

The island nation's low humidity makes it one of the most temperate climates in the world.

Vegetation

The sandy soil on much of the islands has only scrub vegetation.

Some parts of Antigua are more fertile, most notably the central plain, due to the volcanic ash in the soil. These areas have some tropical vegetation and are good for agriculture.

The planting of acacia, mahogany, and red and white cedar on Antigua has led to as much as 11 per cent of the land becoming forested, helping to conserve the soil and water.

Economy

Tourism dominates the economy, accounting for more than half of the gross domestic product (GDP).

Antigua is famous for its many exclusive luxury resorts. But weak tourist activity since early 2000 has slowed the economy.

Investment banking and financial services also constitute an important part of the economy. Major world banks with offices in Antigua include the Bank of America (Bank of Antigua), Barclays, the Royal Bank of Canada (RBC) and Scotia Bank.

Financial-services corporations with offices in Antigua include PriceWaterhouseCoopers.

But the island nation's reputation as a financial centre has also been tarnished by accusations of improprieties. The US Securties and Exchange Commission (SEC) has accused the Antigua-based Stanford International Bank owned by Texas billionaire Allen Stanford of orchestrating a huge fraud which may have bilked investors of some $8 billion, according to a report in March 2010.

The twin-island nation's agricultural production is focused on its domestic market and constrained by a limited supply of water and a labour shortage. The shortage of labour in the agricultural sector is attributed to higher wages in tourism and in the construction industry which attract a large number of workers who could have gone into agriculture. About one-third of all tourists come from the United States.

Manufacturing is made up of enclave-type assembly for export, the major products being bedding, handicrafts and electronic components.

Unlike in many parts of the Third World, the economy of Antigua and Barbuda_ is service-based, with tourism and government services representing the key sources of employment and income.

Tourism accounts directly and indirectly for more than half of the entire gross domestic product. It's also the principal earner of foreign exchange.

However, a series of destructive hurricanes since 1995 resulted in serious damage to the tourist infrastructure, causing a sharp decline in the number of visitors to the island nation.

Also, in 1999 the budding offshore financial sector was seriously hurt by financial sanctions imposed by the United States and the United Kingdom as a result of the loosening of its money-laundering controls.

To lessen its vulnerability to natural disasters, the island nation is making an effort to diversity its economy. Transport, communications and financial services are becoming increasingly important.

Antigua and Barbuda is a member of the Eastern Caribbean Currency Union (ECCU). The Eastern Caribbean Central Bank (ECCB) issues a common currency, the East Caribbean dollar, for all the members of the ECCU.

The ECCB also manages monetary policy, and regulates and supervises commercial banking activities in its member countries.

Antigua and Barbuda also belongs to the predominantly English-speaking Caribbean Community (CARICOM).

Economic history

Before the islands were colonised by Europeans, several Amerindian groups inhabited Antigua and Barbuda, living at the subsistence level.

British colonists established settlements in the islands in 1632. After fighting off the Caribs, the Dutch, and the French to stabilise their colonies, the British settlers grew tobacco, indigo, cotton and ginger as cash crops. As on many other Caribbean islands, sugar cultivation became the most profitable enterprise, quickly surpassing other crops in economic importance.

Due to the vast tracts of land needed for large-scale sugar production, rain forests on the islands were destroyed. Timber from the rain forests was used in shipbuilding and repair.

With the shift to a plantation economy, slaves were imported from Africa. Most of them came from West Africa.

Even after the abolition of slavery in 1834, former slaves continued to work in servitude because of the laws which were designed to keep them in that condition in order for them to provide cheap labour for the plantations. But as the sugar industry began to wane, the plantation economy came to an end.

Primary industries

Agriculture

About 30 per cent of the land on Antigua is suitable for cultivation. But only 18 per cent is being used. Cotton is a profitable export crop. And a modest amount of sugar is harvested every year. There are also plans for production of ethanol from sugarcane.

Vegetables including beans, carrots, cabbage, cucumbers, plantains, squash, tomatoes, and yams are grown mostly on small family plots for local consumption. Some are sold on local markets.

Since 1980, agriculture's contribution to the gross domestic product (GDP) has fallen from more than 40% to 12%.

The decline in the sugar industry left 60% of the country's 66,000 acres under government control, and the ministry of agriculture is encouraging self-sufficiency in order to reduce the need to import food. About 25% of all imports is food.

Crop cultivation is seriously affected by droughts and insects. Cotton and sugar production is curtailed because of soil depletion and the unwillingness of many people to work in the fields.

Mangoes are also an important of the economy, with

more than 1,000 tons harvested every year.

Animal husbandry

The livestock sector is also very important to the economy of the island nation. The country has large numbers of goats and other domestic animals. In 2004, there were 14,300 heads of cattle, 19,000 sheep, 36,000 goats, and 5,700 hogs.

Most of the livestock is owned by individual households.

Milk production in 2004 was an estimated to be 5,350 tons. The government has sought to increase grazing space and to improve stock, breeding Nelthropp cattle and Black Belly sheep. There is also a growing poultry industry.

Fishing

Most fishing is for local consumption, although there is a growing export of the lobster catch to the United States and of some fish to Guadeloupe and Martinique. Antiguans annually consume more fish per capita than any other nation or territory in the Caribbean.

The main fishing waters are near shore or between Antigua and Barbuda.

The country also has shrimp and lobster farms, and the Smithsonian Institution has a Caribbean king crab farming facility for the local market. The government has encouraged modern fishing methods and supported mechanization and the building of new boats.

Forestry

About 11% of the land is forest, mainly red cedar, white cedar, mahogany, and acacia. A reforestation programme was started in 1963, linked with efforts to improve soil and water conservation.

Mining

The island nation has few minerals. Limestone, building stone, clay and barite were exploited until recently.

Limestone and volcanic stone have been extracted from Antigua for local construction. And the manufacture of bricks and tiles from local clay has begun on a small scale.

Barbuda produces only a small amount of salt. And the island of Redonda has phosphates which have been collected through the years but not in very large quantities to justify large-scale commercial exploitation.

Secondary Industries

Industrial activity has shifted from the processing of local agricultural products to consumer and export industries using imported raw materials.

Industrial products include rum, refined petroleum, paints, garments, furniture and electrical components. The government encourages investment in manufacturing industries and most of them have some government participation.

Industry accounted for 19% of GDP in 2001. Manufacturing—which accounts for approximately 5% of GDP—comprises enclave-type assembly for export with major products being bedding, handicrafts, and electronic components.

Prospects for economic growth depend on income growth in the industrialized world, especially in the United States, which accounts for about half of all tourist arrivals. The industrial park located in the Coolidge Area produces a range of products such as paints, furniture, garments, and galvanized sheets, mainly for export.

Tertiary industries

Tourism

Tourism is the mainstay of the economy of Antigua and Barbuda. It's also the leading sector in terms of providing employment and creating foreign exchange. In 1999 it contributed 60 per cent of GDP and more than half of all jobs.

According to the *Americas Review* 1998, tourism contributed 15 per cent directly and around 40 percent indirectly to the GDP in 1998. Real growth in this sector has moved from an average of 7 per cent for the period 1985-89 to 8.24 per cent for the period 1990-95. There was slow growth between 1995 and 1998.

Figures released by the East Caribbean Central Bank (ECCB) in 2000 show that total visitor arrivals increased steadily from 470,975 in 1995 to 613,990 in 1998. In 1999 total visitor arrivals declined by about 4.1 per cent to 588,866, yet the number of visitors staying at least 1 night or more increased by 1.9 per cent over 1998 to total 207,862.

Arrivals via cruise ships in 1999 dropped to 325,195, a fall of 3.4 percent over 1998. The fall-off in cruise passengers was mainly the result of one of the larger cruise ships being out of service for a brief period.

Most of the tourists in 1999 came from the United Kingdom and the United States.

Visitor expenditures have increased steadily since 1990, with total expenditures of EC$782.9 million.

To combat increasing competition from other Caribbean destinations, the government and the Antigua Hotel and Tourist Association have established a joint fund to market the country's appeal as a tourist destination. The Association has agreed to match the proceeds from a 2 per cent hotel guest levy introduced by the government.

At the start of March 2001, the Antigua Workers Union (AWU), the trade union which represents close to 7,000 workers in the tourism industry, described tourism as an industry in crisis.

The AWU claimed the industry is on the decline because some airlines are pulling out of the country, and government was not spending enough money to promote tourism. While the government has conceded that it was not spending enough on marketing because of cash flow problems, it has rejected the AWU's contention that the industry is in crisis.

Financial services

Antigua and Barbuda is advertised as "an attractive offshore jurisdiction."

The country was the first to sign the United Nations' anti-money laundering act. This agreement came out of a conference in 1999 which urged worldwide offshore financial centres to introduce laws to tighten their policing of money laundering activities.

The United Kingdom exerted considerable pressure on Antigua and Barbuda to reform laws to combat money laundering, even issuing an advisory in April 1999 to British financial institutions that Antigua and Barbuda's anti-money laundering laws were wanting.

Antigua and Barbuda responded to this concern, and a subsequent joint United States and United Kingdom review reported they were satisfied that the country had taken positive steps to check illegal activity in this sector. In September 2000 the government of Antigua and Barbuda announced that it had strengthened its surveillance of money laundering and drug trafficking.

In March 2009, the Stanford Financial Group based in Antigua was found by regulators there and in the United

States to be operating a massive ponzi scheme. The international bank controlled by the Stanford group is now (in 2010) in receivership pending the outcome of an investigation.

Retail

The retail sector is dominated by the sale of food and beverages, clothing and textiles, and vegetables. The main markets are located in the capital, St. John's.

There are many street vendors and duty-free shops. The government has been taking steps to improve this sector.

A US$43.5 million vendors' mall and market has been built to provide better facilities for retailers in the capital. In addition, a US$27 million fisheries complex now provides improved facilities for fish processing and retailing.

A growing area of computer business on Antigua is Internet casinos.

Demographics

Ethnicity and racial make-up

Antigua has a population of 85,632, mostly made up of people of West African, British and Portuguese descent.

The ethnic/racial distribution consists of 91% Black, Mulatto and mixed Black/Amerindian; 4.4% other mixed race; 1.7% White; and 2.9% other (primarily East Indian and Asian).

Most Whites are of Irish or British descent.

Christian Levantine Arabs (mostly from Syria, Lebanon and Palestine), Portuguese, and a small number of Asians and Sephardic Jews make up the remainder of the population.

Through they years, there has also been an assertion of identity which has assumed racial characteristics. This has particularly been the case since the latter part of the 20th century. Black identity has been the most prominent.

Behind the late 20th-century revival and redefinition of the role of Afro-Antiguans and Barbudans in the society's cultural life is a history of racial/ethnic tensions which systematically excluded non-Whites.

Within the colonial framework established by the British soon after their initial settlement of Antigua in 1623, five distinct and carefully ranked racial/ethnic groups emerged.

At the top of this social structure were the British who justified their hegemony with arguments of white supremacy and civilising missions.

Amongst these racial and social stratifications were divisions between British Antiguans and non-creolised Britons, with the latter coming out on top.

In short, this was a racial/ethnic hierarchy which gave maximum recognition to people and cultural practices of Anglican origin.

Immediately below the British were the mulattos, a mixed-race group of Afro-European origin. Mulattos, lighter in shade than most Africans, developed a complex system based on skin shade to distinguish themselves from the latter and to legitimise their claims to higher status. In many ways, their attitudes paralleled the British white supremacy ideology.

In the middle of this social stratification were the Portuguese, 2,500 of whom migrated as workers from Madeira, a Portuguese island off the Moroccan coast, between 1847 and 1852 because of a severe famine there. Many established small businesses and joined the ranks of the mulatto class.

The British never really considered the Portuguese as whites and did not allow them into their ranks. Amongst Antiguans and Barbudans of Portuguese descent, status differences were based on the varying degrees of assimilation into the dominant group's Anglicised practices.

Next to the bottom were Middle Easterners who began migrating to Antigua and Barbuda around the turn of the 20th century. Starting as itinerant traders, they soon worked their way into the social mix. Although Middle Easterners came from a variety of areas, as a group they are usually referred to as Syrians. It's obvious that all of them did not come from Syria.

Afro-Antiguans and Afro-Barbudans were at the bottom. Forced into slavery, Africans started arriving in Antigua and Barbuda in large numbers during the 1670s. Very quickly, they grew into the largest racial/ethnic group.

Their entry into the local social structure was marked by a profound racialisation. They ceased being Yoruba, Ewe, Igbo, Akan, Mende or Mandingo and became Negroes or Blacks.

In the 20th century, the colonial social structure gradually started to be phased out with the introduction of universal education and better economic opportunities. This process allowed Blacks to rise to the highest echelons of society and government.

In the 1900s, Spanish-speaking immigrants from the Dominican Republic and Afro-Caribbean immigrants from Guyana and Dominique were added to this ethnic mosaic. They have entered at the social structure's bottom; it is still too early to predict their patterns of assimilation and social mobility.

Today, an increasingly large number of Antiguans and Barbudans live abroad, most notably in the United Kingdom where they collectively constitute a group known as Antiguan Britons. A significant number of them also live in the United States and Canada.

A minority of Antiguan residents are immigrants from other countries, particularly from Dominica, Guyana and

Jamaica. There is also an increasing number of immigrants from the Dominican Republic, St. Vincent and the Grenadines and Nigeria.

An estimated 4,500 American citizens also make their home in Antigua and Barbuda, making their numbers one of the largest American populations in the English-speaking Eastern Caribbean.

Religion

Seventy-four percent of Antiguans are Christians, with the Anglican denomination (about 44%) being the largest. Other Christian denominations are Baptist, Presbyterian, and Catholic.

Non-Christian religions practised in the islands include the Rastafari Movement, Islam, Judaism and the Bahá'í Faith.

Languages

English is the official language, but many of the locals speak Antiguan Creole. The Barbudan accent is slightly different from the Antiguan.

In the years before Antigua and Barbuda's independence, Standard English was widely spoken in preference to Antiguan Creole, but afterwards Antiguans began treating Antiguan Creole as a respectable aspect of their culture. Generally, the upper and middle classes shun Antiguan Creole. The educational system discourages the use of Antiguan Creole and instruction is done in Standard (British) English.

Many of the words used in the Antiguan dialect are derived from British as well as African languages. This can be easily seen in phrases such as: "Me nah go" meaning "I am not going."

Another example is: "Ent it?" meaning "Ain't it?" which is itself dialectical and means "Isn't it?"

Common island proverbs and other sayings often can be traced to Africa.

Culture

The culture is predominantly British: For example, cricket is the national sport and Antigua has produced several famous cricket players including Sir Vivian Richards, Anderson "Andy" Roberts, and Richard "Richie" Richardson.

Other popular sports include football. boat racing and surfing. The Antigua Sailing Week attracts locals and visitors from all over the world.

American popular culture and fashion also have a heavy influence on the island nation.

Most of the country's media is made up of major United States networks.

Antiguans pay close attention to American fashion trends, and major designer items are available at boutiques in St. John's and elsewhere, although many Antiguans prefer to make a special shopping trip to St. Martin, North America, or San Juan in Puerto Rico.

Family and religion play an important roles in the lives of Antiguans. Most attend religious services on Sunday, although there is a growing number of Seventh-day Adventists who observe the Sabbath on Saturday.

The national Carnival held each August commemorates the abolition of slavery in the British West Indies, although on some islands, Carnival may celebrate the coming of Lent. Its festive pageants, shows, contests and other activities are a major tourist attraction. Calypso and soca music are important in Antigua and Barbuda.

Maize and sweet potatoes play an important role in Antiguan cuisine. For example, a popular Antiguan dish, Dukuna (DOO-koo-NAH) is a sweet, steamed dumpling made from grated sweet potatoes, flour and spices.

One of the Antiguan staple foods, fungi (FOON-ji), is a

cooked paste made of maize meal and water.

Cuisine of Antigua and Barbuda

The national dish of Antigua and Barbuda is fungie (pronounced "foon-jee") and pepper pot. Fungie is a dish very similar to the Italian Polenta and is almost completely made from maize meal.

Other local dishes include ducana, seasoned rice, saltfish and lobster (from Barbuda). There are also local confectionaries which include sugar cake, fudge, raspberry and tamarind stew and peanut brittle.

Although these foods are indigenous to Antigua and Barbuda and to some other Caribbean countries, the local diet has diversified and now include the local dishes of Jamaica (e.g. jerk pork), Guyana (e.g. Roti) and other Caribbean countries.

Chinese restaurants have also begun to become more mainstream. The supermarkets sell a wide variety of food, from American to Italian. Meals also vary depending on social class.

Lunches in Antigua and Barbuda typically include a starch, like rice/macaroni/pasta, vegetables/salad, an entree (fish, chicken, pork, beef etc.) and a side dish like macaroni pie, scalloped potatoes or plantains.

Local drinks are mauby, seamoss, tamarind juice, raspberry juice, mango juice, lemonade, coconut milk, hibiscus juice, ginger beer, passion fruit juice, guava juice soursop juice, ginger beer and others.

Adults prefer beer, malt and rum, many of which are made locally. They include Wadadli beer, which is named after the original name of Antigua island, and the award winning English Harbour Rum.

Sunday is the main day most people go to church. It's also the day when the island nation's culture is mostly reflected in the food.

For breakfast one might have salt fish, eggplant (also known as troba), eggs and lettuce. Dinner on Sundays is eaten earlier (around 2:00 pm) because parents are usually off from work and can stay home and cook.

Dinner may include pork, baked chicken, stewed lamb, or turkey, alongside rice (prepared in a variety of ways), macaroni pie, salads, and a local drink.

Dessert may be ice cream and cake or an apple pie (mango and pineapple pie in their season) or Jello.

Music of Antigua and Barbuda

Antigua and Barbuda is a second home for many of the pan-Caribbean genres of popular music and has produced stars in calypso, soca, steel drum, zouk and reggae. Of these, steel drum and calypso are the most integral parts of modern Antiguan popular music. Both styles are imports from the music of Trinidad and Tobago.

The population of Antigua and Barbuda is mostly descended from West Africans brought to the Caribbean as slaves. Thus, the music of Antigua and Barbuda is largely African in character and has only felt a limited influence from European styles.

Unfortunately, very little research has been undertaken on the music of Antigua and Barbuda.

History

Documented music in Antigua and Barbuda began only with the discovery of Antigua by Christopher Columbus in 1493. The island was then populated by the indigenous Arawaks and Caribs.

The islands' early music, however, remains little studied. In the 1780s, documentation exists for African workers participating in outdoor dances accompanied by the *banjar* (later *bangoe*, perhaps related to the banjo) and *toombah* (later *tum tum*), a drum decorated with shell and tin jingles.

By the 1840s, sophisticated subscription balls were common, held biweekly with European-derived quadrilles accompanied by fiddle, tambourine and triangle.

Colonial era churches and missionary activity displaced and otherwise influenced the music of the African slaves who adopted elements of European-derived religious music. The bass bands of the Salvation Army are an important example.

In the mid- to late 19th century, a number of Portuguese indentured workers came to Antigua, bringing with them their styles of music. When most of the Portuguese left in the 1880s, Lebanese music was brought to the island by the immigrants from their native country of Lebanon.

Folk music

During the period of French colonial rule, African slaves were prohibited from celebrating in Carnival. But they continued to do so, secretly, at home. There, an Afro-Caribbean style of percussion, dance and song called benna developed. Later, Antiguan and Barbudan folk music became more dominated by Trinidadian calypso and steelpan.

Most forms of modern Antiguan and Barbudan music are not indigenous to the islands and were imported from France, the United Kingdom, United States, Jamaica and Trinidad.

Colonial dance styles like the highland fling and the quadrille remain popular in Africanised form.

The loss of Antiguan traditions can be ascribed to the lack of a French colonial past (French islands of the Lesser Antilles retain a lot of African-derived music and dance), the influence of the powerful Codrington family, a relatively unified African ethnic identity, the lack of African immigration after the peak of slavery importation, the British military presence at Shirley Heights, and a modern history of an unstable economy and a weak and unstable government.

Old-time Christmas Festival

The Old-Time Christmas Festival was a culturally significant celebration replaced by a Trinidadian-inspired Carnival in 1957. The Antiguan Christmas Festival included several elements that have been incorporated into the modern Carnival

Christmas Festival traditions include both music and dance, especially related to masquerades and iron bands. The highland fling is a common Christmas Festival dance, also played in the modern Carnival, performed by people wearing Scottish kilts, masks made of wire and bearing whips of cowhide.

Dancers wearing banana leaves and animal horns took part in the John Bull, while carolers paraded with long poles covered in lanterns, called *carol trees*, singing with accompaniment by the concertina.

Stilt dancers in robes, called the *Moko jumbie*, *Jumpa-Ben* or *Long Ghosts*, were also common, and were accompanied by kettle and bass drums, fife, triangle (*cling-a-ching*) and the boom pipe made from a plumbing joint one meter long.

Benna

Benna (or *bennah*) is an uptempo Antiguan folk song that was introduced following the prohibition of slavery. Songs usually focused on scandalous and bawdy rumours and gossip and were in a call-and-response form with a leader and an audience. Benna's popularity and similarity to calypso helped make the island receptive to that genre's introduction.

The modern performer, Short Shirt, has attempted to

revive the benna in modern years with his 1977 album *Harambee*, an influential work that began updating benna with social and political awareness.

By the beginning of the 20th century, benna had become a method of folk communication, disseminating news and reports from across the island.

In the 1940s and 50s, an improvisational benna singer named John "Quarkoo" Thomas sang up-to-date stories on legal scandals, and the sexual affairs of the upper-class. He was eventually imprisoned because of the lyrics to "Cocoatea," which was about the daughter of a respected citizen and her secret pregnancy while in a convent.

Popular music

In other popular genres of music, Antigua is best known for the oldest and most successful soca band, the Burning Flames, who have claimed the road march title for many years.

Another well-known Antiguan musician was Patrick "Johnny" Gomes who worked for the calypso giant Mighty Swallow, among many others.

The most famous indigenous musician in Antigua and Barbuda may be Oscar Mason whose son, O'Neill, is also a noted trombonist.

One well-known group, The Antigua Community Players, has been active for more than 52 years, performing a variety of musical productions in many styles including the Antiguan folk song, *benna*.

Other famous indigenous musicians from Antigua/Barbuda are Rawden Edwards (keyboards), and jazz recording artists Roland Prince (guitarist), Courtney Winter (saxophonist), Wendell Richardson, a former guitarist of Osibisa, and world jazz vocalist Charmain Bailey.

Country recording artists Billy Rose and Wayne Daniel were also born on the island of Antigua.

Additionally, Basill Hill, owner of King Midas Records in New York, built a large international nightclub called the Atmosphere in 1978, creating a direct outlet for Antigua and Barbudan singers and bands.

Elements of non-Antiguan and Barbudan music have continued to be imported to the islands in the latter 20th century, including the electronic gospel music of the American Baptist church, and the Afro-Jamaican drumming of Rastafarian music.

Antigua Carnival

The Antiguan Carnival is a celebration of music and dance held annually from the end of July to the first Tuesday in August.

The most important day is that of the *j'ouvert* (or *juvé*), in which brass and steel bands perform for much of the island's population.

Barbuda's Carnival, held in June, is known as Caribana.

When the Antiguan and Barbudan Carnivals replaced the Old-Time Christmas Festival in 1957, it was hoped that they would inspire and promote tourism in Antigua and Barbuda. And some elements of the Christmas Festival remain in the modern Carnival celebrations.

It's a ten-day festival of colorful costumes, beauty pageants, talent shows, and especially good music.

The festivities, which celebrate emancipation range from the Party Monarch and Calypso Monarch competitions of Calypsonians, the Panorama steel band competition, and the spectacular Parade of Bands to the Miss Antigua Pageant and the Caribbean Queen's Competition. In addition to these major events, the nonstop revelry of this eleven-day carnival includes innumerable smaller festivities including local concerts, food fairs, parades and cultural shows.

History of Carnival

For the history of the festival, you have to step back in time to 1 August 1834 when slavery was abolished.

People immediately celebrated by taking to the streets to celebrate their freedom and express their joy and happiness.

Over the years there was a return to this informal celebration until 1957 when the Old-Time Christmas Festival, a festival of much cultural significance, was replaced in 1957 by a Trinidadian-inspired Carnival.

There are several different musical forms featured during Carnival. Calypso, the oldest, has its roots in slavery; a common explanation of its origins is that it began as a way for slaves, who were forbidden to speak in the fields, to communicate with each other.

It is a polyglot, improvisational form that depends largely upon the skill of a soloist, (the calypsonian) who weaves the sounds of many cultures into a lyrical whole. Calypso competitions have long been a highlight of Carnival.

Steel drum music was created when the bamboo percussion instruments traditionally used to back up calypso were replaced by hammered steel pans cut from oil drums.

Whereas there is no dispute that the steel pan was developed in Trinidad, the indigenous development of the steel band in Antigua and Barbuda was an outgrowth of the iron bands which were prominent at Christmas time. Steel drum music has been an important part of Carnival since that time, and Antigua is home to many of the Caribbean's finest steel bands.

Soca is a musical form that grafts the slower beat of American soul music to the upbeat tempos of calypso. Soca began in the 1970s, and by the middle of the 1980s it had become an integral feature of Carnival.

Parades and Mas'

Opening Parade and Ceremony

Antigua's carnival officially kicks off with an opening parade through the city of St. John's. Bands and troupes come out in T-shirts bearing the insignia of their respective companies. Floats, which were big in the past, have begun to see a resurgence in their popularity. The participants of various competitions also make a strong appearance in the Opening parade.

The typical parade route is usually like the following: *The Parade will begin at 3:00 pm from Parliament Drive, and turn unto Queen Elizabeth Highway. From there it will turn right onto Independence Drive, left onto Redcliffe Street continue on until it turns onto Thames Street. From there it will move up High Street, back onto Independence Drive, around the round-about by government house and then finally into Carnival City through the north gate.*

The parade concludes at "Carnival City," the official title given to the Antigua Recreation Ground during the carnival season.

There the opening ceremony follows and the contestants for the various carnival competitions make a final public appearance before their shows. The opening ceremony usually finishes with fireworks.

Children's Carnival

The Children's Carnival parade is set aside so that the children may really enjoy the carnival festivities to the fullest. They march through the streets as well and finish the parade at Carnival City.

The children come out in their costumes and portray

different themes, taken from fairy tales etc.

Cheer leading has also permeated Antigua's carnival.

At Carnival City, the children enter the Prince and Princess competitions. Here each mas troupe enters a boy and girl who wear a costume in the hopes of winning the prince and princess competition. They are having their own fun.

J'ouvert

Like j'ouvert all over the world, Antigua's is characterized by much revelry.

Patrons wake up early like 4 or 5 am and go into St. John's where they find their favorite bands and "jam" with them along the route. There is much beer drinking and painting of the bodies with blue and brown paint. There are also many people who wear colorful costumes.

Carnival Monday and Tuesday

Antigua's carnival festivities conclude on the first Monday and Tuesday in August, dubbed Carnival Monday and Tuesday. They're official holidays.

After J'ouvert on Monday morning, revelers come back into St. John's in the afternoon to march through the town, celebrating.

The troupes, bands and floats all return the very next afternoon to do it again but on a different route. This is dubbed Carnival Tuesday. The parade culminates at Carnival City where different troupes are awarded prizes and the Road March king is chosen.

Music Festival

The Antigua and Barbuda International Music Festival (ABIMF), Romantic Rhythms, is a new addition to the "summer line-up" that climaxes in August at the Carnival celebrations. Geared to becoming a competing counterpart to the Carnival, the ABIMF could eventually become the leading musical event in the entire Caribbean region.

In its first year, the music festival saw some of the world's top artists performing in the show.

Steelpan

The steelpan comes in many different forms and, put together, is called a *steel orchestra*.

Steel bands traditionally are made up of old pieces of metal: old irons, tyre rims, steel pipes and so on.

Antigua's steel orchestras and iron bands can be found in churches and in many villages, and have been popular since their introduction.

Every Carnival is a competition to dub the best band of the island.

Antigua's largest and oldest steel orchestra that still competes is the Hell's Gate steel orchestra.

It is often said that The Brute Force Steel Band was the first steelpan band to record an album anywhere.

Steel Orchestras have evolved to using highly technical instruments costing up to US$1500.00 for one instrument. These pans are meticulously honed out of the steel drum, sunken and burned over a hot fire, chromed and tuned. This process was perfected in Trinidad and Tobago and exported to Antigua & Barbuda through various collaborations between several of the bands in both island-nations.

Calypso

Calypso was sung throughout the English speaking Caribbean, and was used by the poor as a platform for social and political commentary, using complex metaphors and folkloric references to obscure their meaning to outsiders. Later, beginning in the 1960s, a popularized kind of calypso was developed for use in tourist hotels. The first hotel calypsonians were Black Shirt, Skeetch and Dadian who were accompanied by a string ensemble of two guitars and a bass guitar created out of an oil drum.

The Antigua Carnival and the Antiguan Calypso King competition began in 1957. The King that year was Styler.

This era also saw a growth in patriotic calypsos, focused on an emerging sense of victorious nationalism in the wake of growing autonomy.

By the middle of the 1960s, two rival calypsonians dominated the Antiguan scene, Zemaki and Lord Canary. Their conflict was perpetuated as the King Short Shirt and Swallow rivalry during the 1970s and 1980s.

In the middle of the 1980s, the Burning Flames emerged, winning the road march with "Styley Tight" in 1985. They achieved pan-Caribbean acclaim. Antigua and Barbuda's Cultural Heritage.

It is clear that the genre of music we now call Calypso had strong roots in Trinidad and Tobago. But it would be really inaccurate to suggest that this music started in any one island. Every island in the Caribbean has a form of music that resembles "Kaiso" or more commonly referred to as Calypso.

Particularly in the English speaking islands and Belize, our African cultural roots have greatly influenced the beats and form of the music. It is quite amazing to find such similarities across the archipelago. It would perhaps, be more accurate to attribute the Soca genre to Trinidad and Tobago.

The defining staccato bass was the creation of the late Lord Shorty from Barrackpore, Trinidad and Tobago and rose to fame as Lord Shorty with his 1963 hit "Clock and Dagger."

He started out writing songs and performing in the calypso genre. In the 1970s, he began experimenting with calypso by blending it with the local chutney—the music of Trinidad's East Indian population—using instruments such as the sitar and tabla. The style was dubbed "soca".

It is therefore inaccurate to attribute the origin of Calypso to any island. In Belize, they call their variation, "Punta." In Antigua they call theirs,"Benna". what is clear, is that all these musical forms borrow beats from West African Highlife music and have fused North American Pop and R&B with the Latin beats of central and South America and Cuba to form distinct musical genres which have significant variations in islands that were influenced by the French where Zouk and Cadance are popular variations.

Media

There are two daily newspapers, the *Daily Observer* and the *Antiguan Sun* which are also available on other Caribbean islands.

ABS TV 10 is the only television station which shows exclusively local programmes. Many programmes of American television networks are also available on the islands. There are also several local and regional radio stations.

Sports

Cricket is the most popular sport in Antigua and Barbuda.

Football, also known as soccer, is another very popular sport.

Education

The island nation of Antigua and Barbuda has one of the highest literacy rates in the world: more than 90 per cent.

The island of Antigua has two medical schools: the American University of Antigua established in 2004, and the University of Health Sciences Antigua (AUA) founded in 1982.

Other academic institutions include a government-owned state college in Antigua and the Antigua and Barbuda Institute of Information Technology (ABIIT).

The University of the West Indies also has a branch in Antigua.

The island nation also has a number of international schools. The Island Academy International School is the most prominent among them.

Chapter Three:

The Bahamas

THE BAHAMAS is officially known as the Commonwealth of The Bahamas.

The origin of the name "Bahamas" is unclear. It may derive from the Spanish *baja mar*, meaning "shallow seas"; or the Lucayan word for Grand Bahama Island, *ba-ha-ma* "large upper middle land."

It's located in the northeastern part of the Caribbean Sea in the Atlantic Ocean north of Cuba, Hispaniola (an island comprising the Dominican Republic in the east and Haiti in the west), northwest of the Turks and Caicos Islands, and southeast of the United States near the state of Florida.

It has an area of 5,382 square miles and consists of 29 islands, 661 cays, and 2,387 islets or rocks. It's slightly larger than the American states of Connecticut and Rhode

Island combined and had an estimated population of 330,000 in 2010. Its capital is Nassau.

Originally inhabited by the indigenous Arawakan Taino, The Bahamas were the site of Columbus' first arrival in the New World in 1492.

Although the Spanish never colonised The Bahamas, they shipped the native Lucayans (as the Bahamian Taino settlers referred to themselves) to slavery in Hispaniola. The islands were mostly deserted from 1513 to 1650 when British colonists from Bermuda settled on the island of Eleuthera.

The Bahamas became a crown colony in 1718 when the British clamped down on piracy. Following the American War of Independence, thousands of pro-British loyalists and enslaved Africans moved to The Bahamas and set up a plantation economy.

The slave trade in the British empire was abolished in 1807 and many Africans liberated from slave ships by the Royal Navy were settled in The Bahamas during the 19th century. Slavery itself was abolished in 1834 and the descendants of enslaved and liberated Africans form the bulk of the population of The Bahamas today.

History

It's believed that Christopher Columbus's first arrival on land in the New World was on an island which is today known as San Salvador Island. It's also called Watling's Island. It's located in the southeastern part of The Bahamas.

Other historians contend that Columbus landed on Samana Cay, also in the southeastern part of the island nation. This theory is also based on calculations made in 1986 by *National Geographic* writer and editor Joseph Judge. He reached this conclusion based on Columbus's log. But evidence in support of this theory remains inconclusive.

Columbus made first contact with the indigenous Lucayans and exchanged goods with them.

The Spaniards who followed Columbus depopulated the islands, carrying most of the indigenous people off into slavery. The Lucayans throughout The Bahamas were wiped out by exposure to diseases, including smallpox, brought by Europeans and to which they had no immunity. The smallpox epidemic which ravaged the indigenous people after Columbus's arrival wiped out half of the population in what is now The Bahamas.

It is generally assumed that the islands were uninhabited by Europeans until the mid-17th century. However, recent research suggests that there may have been attempts by different groups of people from Spain, France, and Britain, as well as by other Amerindians to settle on the islands.

In 1648, the Eleutherian Adventurers migrated from Bermuda to The Bahamas. They were English Puritans who established the first permanent European settlement on an island which they named Eleuthera. The name is derived from the Greek word for freedom. They later settled on New Providence and named the island Sayle's Island after one of their leaders. To survive, the settlers resorted to using salvaged goods from ship wrecks.

In 1670, King Charles II granted the islands to the Lords Proprietors of the Carolinas who rented the islands from the king with rights of trading, collecting tax, appointing governors, and administering the country.

Eighteenth Century

During proprietary rule, The Bahamas became a haven for pirates including the infamous Blackbeard. To restore orderly government, The Bahamas were made a British crown colony in 1718 under the royal governorship of

Woodes Rogers who, after a difficult struggle, succeeded in suppressing piracy. In 1720 he led local militia to drive off a Spanish attack.

During the American War of Independence, the islands were a target for American naval forces under the command of Commodore Ezekial Hopkins. The capital of Nassau on the island of New Providence was occupied by US Marines for a fortnight.

In 1782, following the British defeat at Yorktown, a Spanish fleet appeared off the coast of Nassau, which surrendered without a fight.

After American independence, some 7,300 Loyalists and their slaves moved to The Bahamas from New York, Florida and the Carolinas. These Americans established plantations on several islands and became a political force in the capital. The small population became mostly African from this point on.

The British abolished the slave trade in 1807. The abolition of the slave trade led to the forced settlement on Bahamian islands of thousands of Africans liberated from slave ships by the Royal Navy. Slavery itself was finally abolished in the British empire on 1 August 1834.

Twentieth Century

Modern political development began after the Second World War. The first political parties were formed in the 1950s and the British made the islands internally self-governing in 1964, with Roland Symonette of the United Bahamian Party as the first premier.

In 1967, Lynden Pindling of the Progressive Liberal Party became the first black premier of the colony, and in 1968 the title was changed to prime minister.

In 1973, The Bahamas became fully independent but retained membership in the commonwealth of Nations. Sir Milo Butler was appointed the first black governor-general (the representative of Queen Elizabeth II) shortly after independence.

Based on the twin pillars of tourism and offshore finance, the Bahamian economy has prospered since the 1950s. However, there remain significant challenges in areas such as education, health care, international narcotics trafficking and illegal immigration from Haiti.

Geography

The closest island to the United States is Bimini which is also known as the gateway to The Bahamas.

The island of Abaco is to the east of Grand Bahama. The southeastern-most island is Inagua. The largest island is Andros Island.

Other inhabited islands include Eleuthera, Cat Island, Long Island, San Salvador Island, Acklins, Crooked Island, Exuma and Mayaguana.

Nassau, the capital city of The Bahamas, lies on the island of New Providence. It's also the largest city in the country.

All the islands are low and flat, with ridges that usually rise no more than 49 to 66 feet. The highest point in the country is Mount Alvernia, formerly called Como Hill, which has an altitude of 207 feet on Cat Island.

To the southeast, the Turks and Caicos Islands and three more extensive submarine features called Mouchoir Bank, Silver Bank, and Navidad Bank are geographically a continuation of The Bahamas. But they're not part of the Commonwealth of The Bahamas.

Climate

The Bahamas are a group of about 700 atolls and cays in the western Atlantic Ocean, of which only between 30 and 40 are inhabited.

The largest of the islands is Andros Island located 120

miles southeast of Florida. The Bimini islands are to its northwest. To the North is the island of Grand Bahama, home to the second-largest city in the country, Freeport. The island of Great Abaco is to its east.

In the far south is the island of Great Inagua, the second-largest island in the country.

The land on The Bahamas is primarily either rocky or mangrove swamp. Low scrub covers much of the surface area.

Pineyards are found on four of the northern islands: Grand Bahama, Great Abaco, New Providence, and Andros.

On some of the southern islands, low-growing tropical hardwood flourishes.

Although some soil is very fertile, it is also very thin. Only a few freshwater lakes and just one river, located on Andros Island, are found in The Bahamas.

The climate of The Bahamas is subtropical to tropical and is moderated significantly by the waters of the Gulf Stream, particularly in winter. Conversely, this often proves very dangerous in the summer and autumn when hurricanes pass near or through the islands. Hurricane Andrew hit the northern islands during the 1992 Atlantic hurricane season, and Hurricane Floyd hit most of the islands during the 1999 Atlantic hurricane season.

While there has never been a freeze reported in The Bahamas, the temperature can fall as low as 35.6–37.4°F during Arctic outbreaks which affect nearby Florida.

Snow was reported to have mixed with rain in Freeport in January 1977, the same time that it snowed in the Miami (Florida) area. The temperature was about 40.1°F at the time.

The climate of the archipelago has two seasons, summer and winter.

During the summer, which extends from May to November, the climate is dominated by warm, moist tropical air masses moving north through the Caribbean.

Midsummer temperatures range from 69.8 to 93.2°F with a relative humidity of 60 to 100%.

In winter months, extending from December to April, the climate is affected by the movement of cold polar masses from North America. Temperatures during the winter months range from 59 to 75.2°F.

Yearly rainfall averages 52 inches and is usually concentrated in the May-June and September-October periods. Rainfall often occurs in short-lived, fairly intense showers accompanied by strong gusty winds which are then followed by clear skies.

Winds are predominantly easterly throughout the year but tend to become northeasterly from October to April and southeasterly from May to September. These winds seldom exceed 24 kilometers per hour except during hurricane season.

Although the hurricane season officially lasts from June to November, most hurricanes in The Bahamas occur between July and October. Before a long lull in activity which ended in the 1990s, the last one to strike was Hurricane David in September 1979. Damage was estimated at US$1.8 million and mainly affected agricultural products.

The most intense twentieth-century hurricane to strike The Bahamas was the 1929 Florida hurricane. Winds of up to 140 miles per hour were recorded. Many lives were lost, and there was extensive damage to buildings, homes, and boats.

Government and politics

The Bahamas is an independent nation. Political and legal traditions closely follow those of the United Kingdom.

It's a parliamentary democracy with two main parties, the Free National Movement and the Progressive Liberal Party.

Tourism provides about half of all jobs. But the number of visitors has dropped significantly since the beginning of the global economic downturn during the last quarter of 2008.

Banking and international financial services also have contracted, and The Bahamas is one of 34 secrecy jurisdictions that would be subject to the Stop Tax Haven Abuse Act introduced in the United States Congress.

The Bahamian archipelago is also a way station for drug smugglers and illegal aliens seeking to enter the United States. And aggressive anti–money laundering efforts have caused some offshore banks to incur losses and leave the country.

The Bahamas is a member of the Commonwealth of Nations. And Queen Elizabeth II is the head of state. She is represented by the governor-general. But the position of governor-general is more symbolic than functional. It's the prime minister who governs the country.

Legislative power is vested in a bicameral parliament which comprises the House of Assembly and the Senate. The House of Assembly carries out all major legislative functions. As under the Westminster system, the prime minister may dissolve parliament and call a general election at any time within a five-year term.

The prime minister is the head of government. He's also the leader of the party which has the largest number of seats in the House of Assembly.

Executive power is exercised by the cabinet. The prime minister choses his cabinet. Cabinet members are drawn from his supporters in the House of Assembly.

The country's largely two-party system is dominated by the centre-left Progressive Liberal Party and the centre-right Free National Movement.

A handful of splinter parties have been unable to win election to parliament. These parties have included the Bahamas Democratic Movement, the Coalition for Democratic Reform and the Bahamian Nationalist Party.

Although The Bahamas is not geographically located in the Caribbean, it is a member of the Caribbean Community.

The judiciary is independent of the executive and the legislature. Jurisprudence is based on English law.

Economy

The Bahamas is one of the most prosperous countries in the Caribbean. Tourism is the backbone of the country's economy. It accounts for over 60 per cent of the Bahamian gross domestic product (GDP) and provides jobs for more than half the nation's labour force.

An example of the vibrancy of the tourism industry is the number of cruise ships which anchor in the nation's capital, Nassau, where tourists visit the straw market to buy different items or have their hair braided.

After tourism, the most important economic sector is financial services, accounting for about 15 percent of the gross domestic product. Offshore banking plays a very important role in the country's economic growth. By December 1998, the government had licensed 418 banks and trust companies in The Bahamas.

The economy has a very competitive tax regime. The government derives its revenue from import tariffs, license fees, property and stamp taxes, but there is no income tax, corporate tax, capital gains tax, value-added tax (VAT), or wealth tax.

Steady growth in tourism and a boom in construction of new hotels, resorts, and residences led to solid GDP growth in recent years, but the slowdown in the American economy and the attacks of 11 September 2001 impeded growth in these sectors in 2001-03.

Manufacturing and agriculture together contribute approximately a tenth of the gross domestic product and show little growth despite government incentives to improve those sectors.

Overall prospects for economic growth depend on the tourism sector whose success is largely determined by what goes on in the American economy. Thats is because the United States is the source of more than 80 per cent of the visitors. For example, more than 5 million tourists visited The Bahamas in 2004. Most of them came from the United States.

Basic Ingredients of the Bahamian Economy

A major contribution to the recent growth in the overall Bahamian economy is Kerzner International's Atlantis Resort and Casino which took over the former Paradise Island Resort. It has provided a much needed boost to the economy.

Also, the opening of Breezes Super Club and Sandals Resort has contributed to economic growth.

The Bahamian government has also adopted a proactive approach to courting foreign investors and has conducted major investment missions to the Far East, Europe, Latin America and Canada.

Agriculture

Agriculture and the fisheries industry together account for 5 per cent of the country's GDP. The Bahamas exports lobster and some fish but does not raise these items commercially.

There is no large-scale agriculture. Most agricultural products are consumed domestically. With few domestic resources and little industry, The Bahamas imports nearly all its food and manufactured goods from the United States. The Bahamas imports about 80 per cent of the food it consumes. But the government is attempting to expand food production to reduce imports and generate foreign exchange. It actively seeks foreign investment aimed at increasing agricultural exports, particularly specialty food items.

American goods and services tend to be favoured by Bahamians due to cultural similarities and heavy exposure to American advertising.

The government officially lists beef and pork production and processing, fruits and nuts, dairy production, winter vegetables, and mariculture (shrimp farming) as the areas in which it wishes to encourage foreign investment.

The Bahamian Government maintains the value of the Bahamian dollar on a par with the American dollar.

And although The Bahamas participates in the political activities of the Caribbean Community (CARICOM), it has not entered into joint economic initiatives with the other Caribbean states which are also members of CARICOM.

The Bahamas has a few notable industrial firms: the Freeport pharmaceutical firm, PFC Bahamas (formerly Syntex) which recently streamlined its production and was purchased by the Swiss pharmaceutical firm Roche; the BORCO oil facility, also in Freeport, which transships oil in the region; the Commonwealth Brewery in Nassau which produces Heineken, Guinness, and Kalik beers; and Bacardi Corp., which distills rum in Nassau for shipment to the United States and European markets.

Other industries include sun-dried sea salt in Great Inagua, a wet dock facility in Freeport for repair of cruise ships, and mining of aragonite from the sea floor at Ocean Cay. Aragonite is a type of limestone with several industrial uses.

The Hawksbill Creek Agreement established a duty-free zone in Freeport, The Bahamas' second-largest city, with a nearby industrial park to encourage foreign industrial investment. The hong Kong-based firm, Hutchison Whampoa, has opened a container port in Freeport.

Agriculture in The Bahamas is carried out on small

plots throughout most of the islands. Only about 1 per cent of the land area is cultivated. The nature of the terrain limits the scope of farming which is mainly a household industry.

The main crops are vegetables: onions, okra and tomatoes. Okra and tomatoes are grown mainly for export. Okra is believed to be of African origin; so is the name okra which from one of the West African languages, perhaps Igbo or Yoruba.

Among the steps the government has taken to expand and improve agriculture is the reserving of 450,000 acres exclusively for farming. About 20,000 of those acres are used to grow fruit.

Export-oriented orange, grapefruit and cucumber production occurs on Abaco.

Agricultural products in 2004 included 55,500 tons of sugarcane, 13,000 tons of grapefruit, 8,700 tons of lemons and limes, 5,000 tons of tomatoes, and 880 tons of sweet potatoes.

Business environment

The Bahamas offers attractive features to the potential investor: a stable democratic environment, relief from personal and corporate income taxes, timely repatriation of corporate profits, proximity to the United States with extensive air and telecommunications links, and a good pool of skilled professional workers.

The government welcomes foreign investment in tourism and banking and has declared an interest in agricultural and industrial investments to generate local employment, particularly in white-collar or skilled jobs.

Despite its interest in foreign investment to diversify the economy, the Bahamian Government responds to local concerns about foreign competition and tends to protect Bahamian business and labor interests. As a result of domestic resistance to foreign investment and high labour costs, growth can stagnate in sectors which the government wishes to diversify.

The country's infrastructure is best developed in the main cities of Nassau and Freeport where there are relatively good paved roads and international airports.

Electricity is generally reliable, although many businesses have their own backup generators.

In Nassau, there are two daily newspapers, three weeklies, and several international newspapers available for sale. There also are eight radio stations.

Both Nassau and Freeport have a television station. Cable TV also is available locally and provides most American programmes with some Canadian and European channels.

Areas of opportunity

The best American export opportunities remain in the traditional areas of foodstuffs and manufactured goods: vehicles; hotel, restaurant and medical supplies; and computers and electronics. Bahamian tastes in consumer products roughly parallel those in the United States. And with approximately 85 per cent of the population being of primarily African descent, there is a large and growing market in the Bahamas for "ethnic" products including personal-care items for hair, skin and many others.

Merchants in southern Florida have found it profitable to advertise in Bahamian publications.

Demographics

Afro-Bahamians

Afro-Bahamians are Bahamians whose ancestry can be traced back to Africa south of the Sahara desert, mostly West Africa.

The first Africans to arrive in The Bahamas came from

Bermuda with the Eleutheran Adventurers as freed slaves looking for a new life. Currently, Afro-Bahamians are the largest ethnic group in the Bahamas. And they have a much higher standard of living than those of previous generations.

Europeans

Euro-Bahamians have their roots in Europe. Most are descendants of British Puritans and American Loyalists who arrived in the Bahamian islands in1649 and 1783, respectively. They constitute 12 per cent of the population and are the largest minority group in the Bahamas.

A small portion of the European Bahamian population are descendants of Greek labourers who were recruited to work in The Bahamas to help develop the sponging industry in the 1900s. They constitute less than 1 per cent of the total population. They have their own highly distinctive characteristics, ethnic and cultural, not shared by the majority of Bahamians, enabling them to preserve their Greek identity and heritage.

There are also white Cubans, Dominicans from Dominican Republic, and Puerto Ricans as well as other smaller minorities.

About two-thirds of Bahamians live on New Providence Island, and about half of the remaining one-third live on Grand Bahama where the second-largest city, Freeport, is located.

The islands were sparsely settled and were a haven for pirates until the late 1700s when thousands of British loyalists and their slaves were given compensatory land grants following the American Revolution. At the turn of the 20th century, the total population of The Bahamas was only 53,000.

The Bahamas has a well-structured educational system. School attendance is compulsory between the ages of five and 16. There are 158 public schools and 52 private schools serving about 70,000 students.

The College of The Bahamas established in Nassau in 1974 provides programmes leading to associate's degrees and bachelor's degrees.

Culture of The Bahamas

In the less developed outer islands, handicrafts include basketry made from palm fronds. This material, commonly called "straw," is plaited into hats and bags that are popular tourist items. Another use is for so-called "Voodoo dolls" even though such dolls are the result of the American imagination and not based on historic fact.

And although not practised by native Bahamians, a form of folk magic called *obeah* derived from West African practices, is common in some Family Islands – out-islands – of The Bahamas mainly because of Haitian migration to those islands. But the practice of obeah is illegal in the Bahamas and punishable by law.

Junkanoo is another cultural practice in The Bahamas. It's a traditional African street parade of music, dance, and art held in Nassau and a few other settlements on Boxing Day and on New Year's Day. Junkanoo is also used to celebrate other holidays and events such as Emancipation Day.

There are also regattas which are important social events in many family island settlements. They usually feature one or more days of sailing by old-fashioned work boats and an onshore festival.

Some settlements have festivals associated with the traditional crop or food of that area, such as the "Pineapple Fest" in Gregory Town in Eleuthera, or the "Crab Fest" on Andros Island.

Other significant traditions include story telling with strong African influence.

Bahamian culture is a hybrid of African and European

cultures.

Though increasingly influenced by commercialisation – due to tourism – and American music and television, Bahamian culture retains much of its uniqueness.

Bahamian culture is related to other creole cultures throughout the Caribbean Basin but also to the Gullah culture in coastal South Carolina and Georgia in the United States. Many Gullah people were taken to the Bahamas after the American Revolutionary War.

Music

Bahamian music has clear connections to African forms. For example, the goombay drums used at junkanoo and goombay festival have been traced to West African djembe drums. And dances such as the fire dance and the ringplay also can be traced to Africa. But the fire dance has become a thing of the past.

Groups like The Baha Men, Ronnie Butler and Kirkland Bodie known for junkanoo music have gained massive popularity in Japan, the United States and elsewhere.

Junkanoo music is indigenous to the Bahamas and is inextricably linked with festivities on Boxing Day and New Year's Day. This traditional celebration started with an African slave named of John Canoe.

Slaves were given a special holiday at Christmas time when they could leave the work of the plantation behind and celebrate.

Parades are characterised by spectacular costumes made of crepe paper and powerful rhythms beaten traditionally on goatskin drums – accompanied more recently with tom-tom drums or bongo drums – as well as rich brass bands and shaking cow bells.

Bahamian music also incorporates other Caribbean forms such as Calypso, Trinidadian Soca and Jamaican Reggae as well as American-inspired Rap and Hip Hop, all of which have African roots.

Calypso and Rake 'n' Scrape singers and bands such as Baha Men have gained great popularity not only in the Caribbean but also in many other parts of the world including the United States and Japan.

Other prominent Bahamian singers include Ronnie Butler, "King" Eric Gibson, K.B. Macklyn, and the Brilanders. They are popular at home and abroad.

Calypso

Calypso is a style of Afro-Caribbean music which originated in Trinidad and Tobago. It has spread in many parts of the Caribbean including the Bahamas.

Soca

Soca is a form of dance music which originated from calypso music. It originally combined the melodic lilting sound of calypso with insistent percussion – which is often electronic in recent music – and local chutney music.

Soca music has evolved through the years since the late seventies and early eighties, given prominence by musicians from various Anglophone Caribbean countries including Trinidad, Guyana, Saint Vincent and the Grenadines, Barbados, Grenada, Saint Lucia, Antigua and Barbuda, The Bahamas, Dominica, Saint Kitts and Nevis, Jamaica, Belize, as well as the United States Virgin Islands.

Junkanoo

Junkanoo was formerly practised in North Carolina in the southern part of the United States and remnants still exist in Belize, Jamaica and Bermuda. In The Bahamas, the most well-known centres of junkanoo are Nassau, Freeport and the Family Islands.

But since the 1950s the influence of American culture has had a profound impact on The Bahamas in many areas including music. This influence comes mainly from television and radio broadcasts beamed from stations in Florida. Also other Caribbean styles have made inroads into The Bahamas. They include calypso, soca and reggae from Trinidad, Jamaica and other islands including Cuba which has its own style of music.

But in spite of all this influence, more traditional Bahamian performers such as Joseph Spence still have enjoyed successful careers playing junkanoo.

Junkanoo's origins are obscure and much-debated. Researchers like E. Clement Bethel have studied the issue extensively, and likely conclusions include that African slaves were allowed celebrations only around Christmas time, and chose to celebrate John Connu, a headman from 18th century Africa. Whether John Connu really ever existed – even the spelling of his last are not Africa – or not will never be known.

Another theory is that the term junkanoo itself has its origin in the functional utility of scrap metal or other objects – junk, hence junkanoo – used to create the distinctive goombay drum.

Similar celebrations once existed across the Caribbean and in North Carolina. But they're now virtually extinct except in The Bahamas and Belize.

In 1973, the year The Bahamas won independence from the United Kingdom, black professionals of the middle and upper classes began to dominate junkanoo celebrations. Costuming and competitions became more complex and commonplace and soon became a tourist attraction.

Aside from being a type of drum, goombay is also percussion music made famous by Alphonso 'Blind Blake' Higgs who for several years played to tourists arriving at Nassau International Airport.

Rake-and-scrape is a unique type of instrumental music made by bending a saw and scraping with a small object, most typically a screwdriver. The music is used to accompany dances derived from European forms like polka and waltz.

Rake-and-scrape's popularity has been declining in recent years but performers such as Lassie Do and the Boys continue to keep the tradition alive.

Christian rhyming spirituals and the *ant'ems* of sponge fisherman are now mostly dead traditions, supplanted by the arrival of pop music.

E. Clement Bethel's master's thesis on traditional Bahamian music was adapted for the stage as *Music of The* Bahamas by his daughter, Nicolette Bethel and Philip A. Barrows. It was first performed at the Edinburgh Festival Fringe in 1991 and was performed for Bahamian audiences in 2002. A recording of the show is available for sale from Ringplay Productions.

Rake and scrape

Rake and scrape music comes from the musical traditions of the Turks and Caicos Islands and is characterized by the use of a saw as the primary instrument. It was brought by immigrants from those islands. The settled on Cat Island and elsewhere in The Bahamas from the 1920s to the 1940s.

Rake and Scrape is traditionally used to accompany the Bahamian Quadrille and the heel-toe polka, both relics of the initial mixture of African and European cultures.

Many of the Turks and Caicos islanders who settled in The Bahamas became some of the most famous musicians in the island nation. And many of them eventually moved back to their homelands, taking with them junkanoo from The Bahamas. Turks and Caicos are now the second most well-known home for junkanoo, surpassed only by The Bahamas.

Ripsaw

Rake-and-scrape music is very closely related to Ripsaw, a musical genre which originated specifically in the Middle and North Caicos in the Turks and Caicos Islands.

Its most distinctive characteristic is the use of the common handsaw as the primary instrument, along with various kinds of drums, box guitar, concertina, triangle and accordion.

The saw is played by scraping an object, usually an old knife blade, along the saw's teeth. The sound is similar to a paper being ripped, and is believed to be the origin of the term *ripsaw*. In contrast to that, *rake-and-scrape* is derived from the method used by a player to create sound from the saw.

Although little is known about ripsaw's genesis, there are two major theories about its origin. One states that the saw was played to imitate the sound of the guido, a Dominican and Haitian accordion. The other theory says Loyalist colonists in the United States brought their African slaves to the islands and invented the ripsaw to imitate the sound of the shekere instrument.

In the Bahamas, Cat Island is the only place where rake-and-scrape is enjoyed and celebrated on a large scale. During June's Labour Day celebration, the island holds a Cat Island Rake and Scrape festival.

Cat Island's rake-and-scrape tradition may be descended from immigrants from Turks and Caicos who moved there in large numbers in the 20th century.

Language

English is the official language of The Bahamas. But a vast majority of the people speak "broken" English known as Bahamian dialect.

There are some minor regional differences from island to island in terms of pronunciation. But, in general, they're all the same.

The second most spoken language in The Bahamas is Haitian creole. It's spoken by 30,000-60,000 Haitian migrants, including a large number of illegal Immigrants.

Religion

The Bahamas is a very religious country. It's often described by Bahamians as "a Christian nation."

In addition to Christianity, the largely hidden and rarely-mentioned practice of *obeah* is said to persist in different parts of the island nation.

A form of witchcraft, *obeah* is sometimes compared with Haitian voodoo. But those who practice it don't call it witchcraft. They call it a religion or a form of religious worship that goes all the way back to Africa.

Storytelling

Storytelling and folklore played a large role in traditional entertainment in Bahamian communities, especially before modern television.

Many of these highly amusing tales are highly instructive, full of wisdom, just as they are in Africa where many if not most of them originated.

For many years, there was a decline in the practice of this important tradition. But it has witnessed a revival through the works of Patricia Glinton Meicholas and other authors.

Few people dispute its African origin. One of the best examples of these stories is ber bookie ber rabbi.

Bush Medicine

Bush medicine has been practised since the arrival of African slaves in the Bahamas. They brought the practice from Africa. And it's still used today.

People afflicted with various diseases are treated using herbs and other plant products. Many plants are similar to those found in Africa because of similar environments. Both, The Bahamas and Africa, have a tropical or subtropical climate.

Chapter Four:

Barbados

BARBADOS is an island nation of the Lesser Antilles. It's 21 miles long and 14 miles wide with an area of 166 square miles.

It is located in the western area of the North Atlantic Ocean, 62 miles east of the Windward Islands and the Caribbean Sea. And within that body of water, it's about 104 miles east of the islands of saint Vincent and the Grenadines, and 250 miles northeast of Venezuela.

The island nation is spared one major scourge: hurricanes. It's located outside the main Atlantic hurricane belt where hurricanes wreak havoc every year.

Once a Portuguese territory known as *os Barbados*, in 1625 it became an English possession in 1625 and later a British colony.

The island nation has a population of about 276,000. At

least 80,000 of them live in or around Bridgetown, the nation's capital and largest city.

Barbados won independence from Britain 1966. It's a member of the Commonwealth of Nations and Queen Elizabeth II is the head of state. Barbados is one of the Caribbean's leading tourist destinations and is the most developed island in the region. It's also the third most developed country in the western hemisphere after the United States and Canada in descending order.

Another name associated with Barbados or her people is "Bim," "Bimshire" and De rock.

The origin of the name Barbados is uncertain but several theories abound. The National Cultural Foundation of Barbados supports the theory of Dr. Richard Allsopp concerning the name's origin.

He contends that "Bim" was a word commonly used by African slaves and that it comes from the phrase "bi mu" – or "bem," "Ndi bem," "Nwanyi ibem" or "Nwoke ibem" – an Igbo phrase meaning "my people."

In colloquial or literary contexts, "Bim" can also take a more deific tone, referring to the "goddess" Barbados.

The words "Bim" and "Bimshire" are recorded in the Oxford English Dictionary and the Chamber's Twentieth Century Dictionaries.

Another possible source for "Bim" is reported to be in the *Agricultural Reporter* of 25 April 1868.

The Reverend N. Greenidge – father of one of the island's most famous scholars, Abel Hendy Jones Greenidge – suggested the listing of "Bimshire" as a county of England. Expressly named were "Wiltshire, Hampshire, Berkshire and Bimshire."

Lastly, the *Daily Argosy* – of Demerara i.e. Guyana – of 1652 referred to "Bim" as a possible corruption of the word "Byam." Byam was a Royalist leader of those opposed to the Parliamentarians.

The *Daily Argosy* suggested that the followers of Byam came to be known as Bims, and the term became a collective name for all Barbadians.

Early history

The first indigenous people in Barbados are thought to be Amerindians from Venezuela.

The Arawak were the second wave of migrants, also from South America. And Caribs arrived from South America in the third wave.

The Portuguese briefly claimed Barbados from the mid-1500s to the 1600s, and may have seized the Caribs on Barbados and used them as slaves. Other Caribs are believed to have fled to neighbouring islands.

Apart from possibly displacing the Caribs, the Portuguese left little impact on the island and by the 1600s left for South America, leaving the island almost uninhabited. Some Arawaks still live in Barbados.

British colonial rule

English sailors who first landed on Barbados in 1625 arrived at the site of present-day Holetown. They took possession of Barbados in the name of King James I.

From the arrival of the first English settlers in 1627–1628 until independence in 1966, Barbados was under uninterrupted British rule and was the only Caribbean island that did not change hands during the colonial period.

In spite of that, Barbados always enjoyed a large measure of local autonomy. Its House of Assembly began meeting in 1639. Among the first important figures in the island's colonial history was Sir William Courten, an Anglo-Dutchman.

Fighting during the War of the Three Kingdoms and the Interregnum spilled over into Barbados and Barbadian territorial waters.

The island was not involved in the war until after the

execution of Charles I when the island's government fell under the control of Royalists. Ironically, the island's governor, Philip Bell, remained loyal to Parliament while the Barbadian House of Assembly under the influence of Humphrey Walrond supported Charles II.

Slavery became a major institution and remained the backbone of the island's economy for centuries. Relations between Africans and whites were strictly regulated by slave codes.

With the increased implementation of those codes which fostered differential treatment between Africans and white workers and planters, the island became increasingly unattractive to poor whites. Black or slave codes were implemented in 1661, 1676, 1682, and 1688.

In response to the codes, African slaves organised several slave rebellions but none succeeded. And an increasingly repressive legal system increased the gap between white indentured servants and black slaves in terms of treatment. Also, imported slaves became much more attractive for the rich planters who would increasingly dominate the island not only economically but also politically.

Nevertheless, poor whites who had or acquired the means to emigrate often did so. Planters expanded their importation of African slaves to cultivate sugarcane.

By the end of the 18th century, the island's demographic composition had changed dramatically. Instead of being mainly English and Scottish-Irish, the population became overwhelmingly black.

Barbados eventually had one of the world's biggest sugar industries after starting sugarcane cultivation in 1640.

One group which was instrumental in ensuring the early success of the sugarcane industry was that of Sephardic Jews who had been expelled from the Iberian peninsula. Many of them ended up in Brazil.

Sugarcane plantations quickly replaced tobacco ones.

Before then, tobacco was the main export. As the sugar industry developed to become the island's main commercial enterprise, Barbados underwent another transformation. Large plantation estates replaced smallholdings of the early English settlers.

Some of the displaced farmers moved to other English colonies in the Americas, most notably North and South Carolina, and British Guiana as well as Panama.

To work on the plantations, white farmers imported slaves from West Africa and other parts of the continent, but mainly from West Africa. Many African slaves were also taken to other Caribbean islands.

The British abolished the slave trade in 1807 but not the institution itself.

In 1816, slaves in Barbados rose up against their masters in the largest major slave rebellion in the island's history. About 20,000 slaves from more than 70 plantations joined the rebellion.

They drove whites off the plantations but widespread killings did not take place.

The uprising came to be known as "Bussa's Rebellion," named after the slave ranger Bussa who with his assistants hated slavery, found the treatment of slaves on Barbados to be "intolerable," and believed the political climate in the United Kingdom provided an opportunity for slaves to peacefully negotiate with their masters for freedom.

Bussa's Rebellion failed. At least 120 slaves died in the uprising or were immediately executed. Another 144 were brought to trial and executed. And the rest of the rebels were shipped off the island and sent elsewhere in the Caribbean. Sending them back to Africa was not an option, although it would have been the best for the sake of peace and justice for the slaves.

Slavery was finally abolished in the British empire eighteen years later in 1834.

In Barbados and the rest of the British West Indian colonies, full emancipation from slavery was preceded by an apprenticeship period that lasted for four years.

In 1884, the Barbados Agricultural Society sent a letter to Sir Francis Hincks requesting his private and public views on whether the Dominion of Canada would favourably entertain having the then colony of Barbados admitted as a member of the Canadian Confederation.

Then in 1952 the *Barbados Advocate* newspaper polled several prominent Barbadian politicians, lawyers, businessmen, the Speaker of the Barbados House of Assembly and later, as first president of the Senate, Sir Theodore Branker, Q.C. and found them to be in favour of immediate federation of Barbados with the rest of the British Caribbean with complete dominion status within five years from the date of inauguration of the West Indies Federation with Canada.

However, plantation owners and merchants of British descent still dominated local politics because of the high income qualification required for voting.

More than 70 per cent of the population, many of them disenfranchised women, were excluded from the democratic process.

And it was not until the 1930s that the descendants of emancipated slaves began a movement for political rights. One of the leaders of this movement, Sir Grantley Adams, founded the Barbados Labour Party (BLP) in 1938, then known as the Barbados Progressive League.

While being a staunch supporter of the monarchy, Adams and his party also demanded more rights for the poor and for the people.

Progress towards a more democratic government was made in 1942 when the exclusive income qualification was lowered and women were given the right to vote. By 1949, government control was wrested from the planters and, in 1958, Adams became premier of Barbados.

From 1958 to 1962, Barbados was one of the ten members of the West Indies Federation, an association doomed – from the beginning – because of nationalist sentiments on the different islands, each harbouring a desire for full independence without any entanglements or restrictions. It was also doomed because its members, as colonies, had only limited legislative power.

Adams served as the federation's first and only "premier." But he failed in his attempts to form similar unions. And his continued defence of the monarchy was used by his opponents as evidence that he was no longer in touch with the needs of his country.

Errol Walton Barrow, a fervent reformer, became the new people's advocate. Barrow had left the Barbados Labour Party (BLP) and formed the Democratic Labour Party (DLP) as a liberal alternative to Adams' conservative government. He instituted many progressive social programmes such as free education for all Barbadians and the school meals system.

By 1961, Barrow had replaced Adams as premier and the DLP took control of the government.

With the dissolution of the federation, Barbados had reverted to its former status as a self-governing colony.

The island sought and negotiated its own independence with the colonial power at a constitutional conference in the United Kingdom in June 1966.

After years of peaceful and democratic progress, Barbados finally became an independent state on 30 November 1966, with Errol Barrow its first prime minister.

Barbados continued to maintain historical ties with Britain by joining the Commonwealth of Nations. A year later, the island nation became a member of the United Nations (UN) and the Organisation of American States (OAS).

Government and politics

Barbados has been an independent country since 30 November 1966. It functions as a constitutional monarchy and parliamentary democracy patterned after the British Westminister system. Although Queen Elizabeth II serves as the head of state, her role is only ceremonial, exercised on her behalf by the governor-general who is Barbadian and resident in Barbados. Real power is in the hands of the prime minister who is the head of government.

Barbados has a two-party system. The two dominant parties are the Democratic Labour Party (DLP) and the Barbados Labour Party (BLP).

The Barbados Labour Party (BLP) once ruled for 16 years from 1993 to 2008.

Barbados has had a number of third parties since Independence: The People's Pressure Movement formed in the early 1970s which contested the 1976 elections; the National Democratic Party which competed in the 1994 elections; and the People's Democratic Congress which participated in the 2008 electoral contest.

In addition to these smaller parties, several independent candidates also ran for office. But no independent candidate has ever won a seat in parliament.

The Democratic Labour Party (DLP) defeated the BLP Barbados Labour Party (BLP) in the last election in 2008. This was a surprise since the BLP had been in power for almost 15 years.

Law

At the time of independence, British law and other measures adopted by the Barbadian parliament became the basis of the modern-day law system.

In Barbados, camouflage clothing is reserved for military use and forbidden for civilians to wear.

Geography

Barbados is the easternmost island of the Lesser Antilles. It's located east of the other West Indies isles.

It's 480 kilometers north of Guyana, 160 kilometers east of St. Vincent, and 965 kilometers southeast of Puerto Rico. It's also roughly 100 kilometers east of its neighbours in the Windward Islands.

It's flat in sharp contrast with neighbouring islands to the west – the Windward Islands.

The island of Barbados rises gently to the central highland region, with the highpoint of the country being Mount Hillaby in Scotland District. The peak is 1,120 feet above sea level.

Much of the country is circled by coral reefs.

Barbados' capital and main city, Bridgetown, is in the parish of Saint Michael.

Other major towns scattered across the island include Holetown in the parish of Saint James; Oistins in Christ Church parish; and Speightstown in the parish of Saint Peter.

Barbados is often spared the worst effects of the region's tropical storms and hurricanes during the rainy season because its far eastern location in the Atlantic Ocean puts it just outside the principal hurricane strike zone.

On average, a hurricane may strike about once every 26 years in Barbados. The last significant hit from a hurricane to cause severe damage to the island nation was Hurricane Janet in 1955.

Barbados has a coastline spanning 60 miles and is fringed with coral reefs. The island itself is characterised by lowlands or gently sloping, terraced plains, separated by rolling hills that generally parallel the coasts.

Elevations in the interior range from 180 to 240 meters above sea level.

Sugarcane is planted on almost 80 per cent of the island's limestone surface. The soils vary in fertility; erosion is a problem, with crop loss resulting from landslides, washouts, and falling rocks.

Most of the small streams are in Scotland District. The

rest of the island has few surface streams; nevertheless, rainwater saturates the soil to produce underground channels such as the famous Coles Cave.

Since 2009 and 2010, members of the private real estate industry in Barbados have been proposing the creation of artificial islands to be anchored off the west coast of Barbados.

According to Paul Altman of Altman Realty, the envisioned plan would consist of two islands: one measuring 250-acres in size and would house new tourism-based developments and upscale boutique shoppes; and the other island would be 50-acres in size and would serve as a open national park. Both proposed islands would be a short distance from the Deep Water Harbour in Bridgetown.

Climate

Located between the Caribbean Sea and the North Atlantic Ocean northeast of Venezuela, Barbados lies within the tropics.

The climate is moderate tropical, with a wet season (June–November) and a more dry season (December–May).

Its generally pleasant maritime climate is influenced by northeast trade winds which moderate the tropical temperature. Cool, northeasterly trade winds are prevalent during the December to June dry season.

The overall annual temperature ranges from 75.2 to 82.4°F; slightly lower temperatures prevail at higher elevations. Humidity levels are between 71 percent and 76 percent year round.

Rainfall occurs primarily between July and December and varies considerably with elevation.

Economy

Since achieving independence in 1966, the island nation of Barbados has transformed itself from a low-income economy dependent upon sugar production into an upper-middle-income economy based on tourism and the offshore sector.

Barbados went into a deep recession in the 1990s after 3 years of steady decline caused by fundamental macroeconomic imbalances. After a painful readjustment process, the economy began to grow again in 1993. Growth rates have averaged between 3%-5% since then.

The country's three main economic sectors are tourism, international business including financial services, and foreign direct-investment. These are partly fuelled by the island nation's advantages as a service-driven economy and as an international business centre.

Pre-independence

Since the first settlement by the British in 1625, the economy of Barbados was primarily dependent on agriculture. During the 1630s, much of the desirable land had been deforested across the entire island. Soon after that, Barbados was divided into large estate-plantations and used indentured labour mainly from the British Isles to grow tobacco and cotton.

Facing stiff competition from the North American colonies and the neighbouring West Indian islands, Barbados switched to the production of sugarcane. Cultivation of sugarcane was quickly introduced by the exiled Jewish community which immigrated into Barbados from Dutch Brazil during the mid-1600s.

The introduction of sugarcane became the single best move for the island's economy during that time. The economy grew fast and Barbados had so many windmills built that it had the second-highest density of windmills per square mile in the world, second only to the Netherlands.

During the next 100 years, Barbados remained the richest of all the European colonies in the Caribbean region because of sugar production.

Prosperity in the colony of Barbados remained unmatched in the region until sugarcane production in the larger countries – especially Haiti and Jamaica, and elsewhere – expanded significantly, surpassing Barbados. But, despite being eclipsed by larger sugar producers, Barbados continued to grow sugarcane on a large scale well into the 1900s. And it continues to do so today.

After slavery ended in the British empire in 1834, many Bajans – as Barbadians are also known – started to place more emphasis on upward mobility and education.

During the 1930s, politicians in Barbados started to demand self-government while also emphasising the need for the island to retain – within the country – profits from its spectacular economic growth. Since the island was still a colony, a lot of the profits were being sent to the United Kingdom by the British government.

As the 1940s-1950s went by, Barbados moved towards developing political ties with neighbouring Caribbean islands. The West Indies Federation was created by Britain for Barbados and nine other Caribbean territories in 1958.

It was an experiment in regional integration reminiscent of the Federation of Rhodesia and Nyasaland – also known as the Central African Federation – formed a few years earlier, also by the British. Both failed and, coincidentally, around the same time.

The West Indies Federation which collapsed in 1962 was first led by the premier of Barbados. Later, Barbados tried to negotiate several other unions with the other islands, yet it became likely that Barbados needed to move on.

The island peacefully negotiated with Britain its own

independence and became a sovereign nation at midnight on 30 November 1966.

Post independence

Following independence from the United Kingdom on 30 November 1966, sugarcane still remained a chief money-maker for Barbados. The island's politicians tried to diversify the economy from just agriculture.

During the 1950s-1960s visitors from both Canada and the United Kingdom started transforming tourism into a huge contributor for the Barbadian economy. The manmade Deep Water Harbour at Bridgetown had been completed in 1961 and, thereafter, the island could handle most modern ships for shipping sugar or handling cargoes at the port facility.

As 1970s progressed, global companies started to recognise Barbados for its highly educated population. In May 1972 Barbados formed its own Central Bank, breaking off from the East Caribbean Currency Authority (ECCA). By 1975, the Barbadian dollar was changed to a new fixed/constant rate of exchange with the US$; the rate being changed to present day US$1 = BDS$1.98 (BDS $1.00 = ~US$0.50).

By the 1980s, a growing manufacturing industry was seen as a considerable earner for the Barbados economy. With manufacturing then being led by companies such as Intel Corporation and others, the manufacturing industry contributed greatly to the economy during the 1980s and early 1990s.

As one of the founding members, Barbados joined the World Trade Organization on 1 January 1995. Following the membership in the WTO, the Government of Barbados aggressively tried to make the island's economy fully WTO compliant. This led to the collapse of much of the manufacturing industry in Barbados during the late 1990s. Many companies like Intel and others moved from

Barbados to lower-cost Asian countries.

During the late 1990s, more companies started to become interested in Barbados' offshore sector; the sector overtook sugar as the new main money earner.

In 1999-2000 the OECD "blacklist" was circulated with Barbados listed in error. The negative fallout stymied new investment in Barbados' offshore sector for nearly 2 years as Barbados authorities acted swiftly, and successfully, proving that the island's economy was regulated sufficiently to ward off financial criminal activity and that it was not a "Tax Haven," as charged, but was instead a low-tax regime.

As the global recession hit in 2001, the offshore sector in Barbados slightly contracted further thereby making tourism the new main money maker, after having earlier eclipsed manufacturing and sugarcane.

The government further changed legislation to transform the island's economy into one which fosters investment. This lead to several new hotel developments, among other investment projects. And the government continues to seek private investment in the economy to sustain and fuel economic growth.

Several large hotel projects such as Port Charles Marina in Speightstown helped tourism continue to expand in 1996-99, as did the Hilton Hotel on Needhams Point, Saint Michael, in 2005.

Various firms provide routine economic analysis of the Barbadian economy. Barbados is the 51st richest country in the world in terms of gross domestic product (GDP) per capita. It has a well-developed mixed economy and a moderately high standard of living. According to the World Bank, Barbados is classified as being in the 66 top high-income economies in the world.

Historically, the economy of Barbados had been dependent on sugarcane production and related activities. But in the late 1970s and early 1980s, the island nation diversified into the manufacturing and tourism.

Offshore finance and information services have become important foreign exchange earners. And there is a healthy light manufacturing sector. The island has seen a boom in construction, with the development and redevelopment of hotels, office complexes, and homes being the most significant.

The economy contracted in 2001 and 2002 due to slowdowns in tourism, consumer spending and the impact of the September 11, 2001 attacks, but rebounded in 2003 and has shown steady growth since 2004.

Traditional trading partners include Canada, the Caribbean Community – especially Trinidad and Tobago – as well as the United Kingdom and the United States.

The public service remains Barbados' largest single employer.

In 2000, economic forecasts showed that Barbados would become the world's smallest developed country by 2008. But they have been revised and now show that the goal is achievable around 2025.

Wages

Barbadians have ranked as being on the high end of wages in the Americas. The only legislated minimum wage in Barbados is for shop assistants, where wages can be no less than BDS$5.00 (~ US$2.50) per hour.

In October 2009, Dr. Delisle Worrell, Executive Director of the Centre for Money and Finance at the University of the West Indies (UWI), Cave Hill Campus in Barbados, stated that "the average Barbadian now earns between BDS$200 and BDS$499 dollars per week..."

Primary industries

Agriculture

About 16,000 hectares (39,500 acres), or 37.2% of the

total land area, are classified as arable. At one time, nearly all arable land was devoted to sugarcane but the percentage devoted to crops for local consumption has been increasing.

Major food crops are yams, sweet potatoes, maize, eddoes, cassava, and several varieties of beans.

Inadequate rainfall and lack of irrigation has prevented the development of other agricultural projects, although some vegetable farming takes place on a commercial scale.

Some cotton is also grown in drier parts of the island. but until cotton can be picked by machine, it is unlikely that output will rise to its former level.

Animal husbandry

Livestock rearing isn't a major occupation in Barbados, mainly because good pasture has always been scarce and imported animal feed is expensive.

The island imports large quantities of meat and dairy products. Most livestock is owned by individual households.

Estimates for 1999 showed 23,000 head of cattle, 41,000 sheep, 33,000 hogs, 5,000 goats, and 4,000,000 chickens.

Poultry production in 1999 included 9,000 tons of meat and 1,000 tons of hen eggs.

Apart from self-sufficiency in milk and poultry, the limited agricultural sector means that Barbados imports large amounts of basic foods, including wheat and meat.

Fishing

The fishing industry employs about 2,000 persons, and the fleet consists of more than 500 powered boats. The catch in 2000 was 3,100 metric tons.

Flying fish, dolphin fish, tuna, turbot, kingfish, and swordfish are among the main species caught. A fisheries terminal complex opened at Oistins in 1983.

Forestry

Fewer than 20 hectares (50 acres) of original forests have survived the 300 years of sugar cultivation.

There are an estimated 5,000 hectares (12,350 acres) of forested land, covering about 12% of the total land area. In 2000, Barbados imported $35.3 million in wood and forest products.

Mining

Deposits of limestone and coral are quarried to meet local construction needs. Production of limestone in 2000 amounted to 1.5 million tons.

Clays and shale, sand and gravel, and carbonaceous deposits provide limited yields.

Oil production is also undertaken in Barbados, with much of the on-shore activity taking place in Woodbourne, Saint Philip.

Secondary industries

Manufacturing

The manufacturing sector in Barbados has yet to recover from the recession of the late 1980s when bankruptcies occurred and almost one-third of the workforce lost their jobs.

The electronics sector in particular was badly hit when the U.S. semi-conductor company, Intel, closed its factory in 1986.

Leaving aside traditional manufacturing such as sugar refining and rum distilling, Barbados's industrial activity is partly aimed at the local market, producing goods such as tinned food, drinks, and cigarettes.

Many industrial estates are located throughout the island. A cement factory is located in St. Lucy.

The export markets have been severely damaged by competition from cheaper Caribbean and Latin American competitors.

But domestic manufacturing also faces serious potential problems as trade liberalisation means that the government can no longer protect national industries by imposing high tariffs on imported goods.

Thus, Barbadian manufacturers must compete with those from other regional economies whose wage costs and other overheads are usually much lower.

The other significant industrial employer is the petroleum sector in places where oil deposits are located in the southern parishes. But oil has never been produced in commercial quantities. The island's small oil refinery was closed in 1998. And refining was moved to Trinidad and Tobago where labour and other costs are cheaper.

Construction

A construction boom, linked to tourism and residential development has assisted the recovery of a large cement plant in the north of the island that was closed for some years and reopened in 1997.

Tertiary industries

Tourism

Tourism is Barbados's crucial economic activity and has been since the 1960s. At least 10 per cent of the working population – some 13,000 people – are employed in this sector which offers a wide range of tourist accommodations from luxury hotels to modest self-catering establishments.

After the recession years, tourism picked up again in

the mid-1990s, only to face another slowdown in 1999. This drop was in part due to increasing competition from other Caribbean countries such as the Dominican Republic, and in part to a reduction in visits from cruise ships as they shifted to non-Caribbean routes or shorter routes such as The Bahamas.

Cruise ship visitors totalled 445,821 in 1999, a reduction from 517,888 in 1997, but stay-over visitors rose to 517,869 in 1999, setting a new record. Overall, the country witnessed over US$700 million in tourism receipts in 1999.

The real problem for Barbados is that tourist facilities are too densely concentrated on the southern coast, which is highly urbanized, while the Atlantic coast, with its rugged shoreline and large waves, is not suitable for beach tourism. Also, there are few large brand-name hotels, which makes marketing the island in the United States difficult.

On the other hand, the absence of conglomerates and package tours results in a far greater trickle-down of tourist spending among the general population.

Due to its relatively high levels of development and its favourable location, Barbados has become one of the prime tourist destinations in the Caribbean.

Numerous internationally-renowned hotels offering world-class accommodation can be found on the island. Time-shares are available, and many of the smaller local hotels and private villas which dot the island have space available if booked in advance.

The southern and western coasts of Barbados are popular, with the calm light blue Caribbean Sea and their fine white and pinkish sandy beaches.

Along the island's east coast, which faces the Atlantic Ocean, there are tumbling waves which are perfect for light surfing. But some areas remain risky due to under-tow currents.

Shopping districts are popular in Barbados, with ample

duty-free shopping.

There is also a festive night-life in mainly tourist areas such as Saint Lawrence Gap.

Other attractions include wildlife reserves, jewelry stores, scuba diving, helicopter rides, golf, exotic drinks, cave exploration, sightseeing, fine clothes shopping, and festivals – the largest being the annual Crop Over festival in July-August.

Informatics

Informatics employed almost 1,700 workers in 1999, about the same number the sugar industry did.

The island has been involved in data processing since the 1980s and now specialises in operations such as database management and insurance claims processing.

Costs in Barbados are higher than elsewhere in the Caribbean – although still only half of costs in the United States – but the island offers strong advantages such as a literate English-speaking labour force and location in the same time zone as the eastern United States.

Despite these factors, employment has fallen in recent years, reflecting increasing mobility on the part of foreign companies which frequently relocate to lower-cost areas.

Financial services

The financial services sector has also faced problems as licences issued to new financial companies have slowed down since 1998.

There are an estimated 47 offshore banks as well as hundreds of other insurance and investment companies, all catering to overseas clients.

In 1998, approximately 7,500 people were employed in the banking and insurance sector.

The financial sector is also under threat of sanctions from the EU and the Organization for Economic Cooperation and Development (OECD), both of which have expressed concerns about money laundering, tax evasion, and other financial improprieties in Caribbean offshore centres.

Retail

Retailing is an important economic activity, especially in Bridgetown where there are large department stores and supermarkets. In the countryside, most stores are small and family-run. Some 18,000 people work in the retail sector.

Transport

Transport on the island is relatively convenient, with "route taxis" called "ZRs" – pronounced "Zed-Rs"– travelling to most points on the island.

These small buses can at times be crowded, as passengers are generally never turned down regardless of the number. However, they will usually take the more scenic routes to destinations.

They generally depart from the capital Bridgetown or from Speightstown in the northern part of the island.

Altogether, there are three bus systems running seven days a week, although less frequently on Sundays: the ZRs; the yellow minibuses; and the blue Transport Board buses. A ride on any of them costs $1.50 BBD.

The smaller buses from the two privately owned systems – "ZRs" and minibuses – can give change; the larger blue buses from the government-operated Barbados Transport Board system can not.

Children in school uniform ride for free on the government buses and for $1.00 on the minibuses and ZRs.

Most routes require a connection in Bridgetown. Some drivers within the competitive privately-owned systems are reluctant to advise persons to use competing services, even if those would be more suitable.

Some hotels also provide visitors with shuttles to points of interest on the island from outside the hotel lobby. There are several locally owned and operated vehicle rental agencies in Barbados but there are no multinational companies.

The island's only airport is the Sir Grantley Adams International Airport (GALA). It receives daily flights by several major airlines from points round the globe, as well as several smaller regional commercial airlines and charters. The airport serves as the main air-transport hub for the Eastern Caribbean. It is undergoing a US$100 million upgrade and expansion.

There is also a helicopter shuttle service which offers air taxi services to a number of sites around the island, mainly on the west coast tourist belt. Air and water traffic is regulated by the Barbados Port Authority.

Demographics

Barbados has a population of about 300,000. About 90 per cent of all Barbadians – also known colloquially as *Bajan* – are of African descent. They're also called "Afro-Bajans."

The remainder of the Barbadian population includes groups of European descent – "Anglo-Bajans"/"Euro-Bajans" – originally from the Great Britain and the Republic of Ireland; Chinese, and Indians from India as well as Pakistanis.

Other groups in Barbados include people from the United Kingdom, the United States and Canada who are not Barbadian.

Barbadians who return to the island after years of residence in the United States and children born in America to Bajan parents are called "Bajan Yankees." But the is considered derogatory by some people.

Barbados is a chief destination for emigrants from Guyana in South America. Guyanese share historical and cultural ties with Barbados. Guyana was also once a British colony. And both countries have large populations of people of African as as well Asian – Indian – descent.

The biggest communities in Barbados besides the black Afro-Caribbean community are:

- Indo-Guyanese. They play an important part in the island's economy and even more so because of increased immigration from Guyana.

There are reports of a growing Indo-Bajan diaspora originating from Guyana and India. They brought soca-chutney, roti and many Indian dishes into Barbadian culture.

Mostly from southern India and Hindu states, the population of these "Desi" people is growing significantly. But it's still smaller than that of their counterparts in Trinidad and Guyana.

- Euro-Bajans constitute about 4 per cent of the population. They have lived in Barbados since the 1500s. They came from England. Ireland and Scotland.

In 1643, there were 37,200 whites in Barbados constituting 86 per cent of the population. They're commonly known as "White Bajans" although some of them have Afro-Caribbean ancestry. Many black Barbadians also have European genes because of inter-racial relationships including marriage.

Euro-Bajans introduced folk music – such as Irish music and and Highland music – to the island. Also names of many places in Barbados are British. They include "Scotland," a mountainous region in Barbados; and "Trafalgar Square" in the island's capital, Bridgetown. Bridgetown's Trafalgar Square was later renamed "Heroes Square."

Among White Barbadians, there exists an underclass known as Redlegs. They're descendants of indentured servants and prisoners brought to the island from Great Britain. But many of them also moved to the United States where they became some of the earliest white settlers in the states of North Carolina and South Carolina.

- Chinese are only a small portion of Barbados' Asian demographics, far smaller than their counterparts in Jamaica and Trinidad. Most of them first arrived in Barbados in the 1940s during the Second World War. They came mainly from what was then the British territory of hong Kong. Many

Chinese food and culture – especially food – is becoming an integral part of Bajan culture.

- Lebanese and Syrians form the Middle Eastern community on the island and make up a small percentage of the country's Muslim population.

The majority of the Lebanese and Syrians migrated to Barbados because of trade opportunities. But their numbers are dwindling because of emigration and immigration to other countries.

Jewish people arrived in Barbados not long after after the first British settlers arrived on the island in 1627. Bridgetown is the home of the oldest Jewish Synagogue in the Western Hemisphere, dating from 1654, though the current structure was erected in 1833 replacing one destroyed by the hurricane of 1831.

Tombstones in the neighbouring cemetery date from the 1630s. Now under the care of the Barbados National Trust, the site was deserted in 1929, but was subsequently saved and restored by the Jewish community in 1983.

- Indians from Gujarat in India make up majority of the Muslim population. Muslim-Indian Barbadians are often perceived to be the most successful group in business, along with the Chinese Bajans; a situation similar to what prevails in East Africa where people of Indian and Pakistani descent – but mostly Indian – are the most prosperous in business in the countries of Kenya, Uganda and Tanzania. I also know this from experience because I lived in Tanzania for 23 years.

The average life expectancy of Barbadians is 77 years for both males and females. Barbados and Japan have the distinction of having highest number of centenarians (on a per capita basis) in the world.

Diaspora

Many Bajans live overseas. The majority migrated – and continue to migrate – to Anglophone countries, especially the United Kingdom, the United States, and Canada.

They make significant financial contributions to the island's economy by sending money back home. They also contribute to the economy when they spend money during visits to the island.

Notable Barbadians include Shirley Chilsom, a congresswoman from New York, who became the first major-party black candidate to run for president of the United States and the first woman to run for the Democratic presidential nomination in 1972.

Languages

English is the sole official language of Barbados. The Standard of English used in Barbados tends to conform to the vocabulary, pronunciations, spellings, and conventions akin to, but not exactly the same as, those of British English.

A regional variant of English, referred to locally as Bajan, is spoken by most Barbadians in everyday life, especially in informal settings. In its full-fledged form, Bajan sounds markedly different from the Standard English heard on the island.

The degree of intelligibility between Bajan and general English varies depending on the speakers' origins and the "rawness" of one's accent. In rare instances, a Bajan speaker may be completely unintelligible to an outside English speaker if sufficient slang terminology is used in a sentence.

Bajan is somewhat differentiated from – but highly influenced by – other Caribbean English dialects; it's a fusion of British English and elements borrowed from the languages of West Africa.

Hindi and Bhojpuri are also spoken on the island by a small Indo-Bajan minority.

Spanish is considered the most popular second language on the island, followed by French.

Religion

In religion, most Barbadians of African and European descent are Christians, mainly of the Anglican Church.

The Church of England was the official state religion until its legal disenfranchisement by the Parliament of Barbados following independence.

Religious minorities include members of Protestant churches, Hindus, Muslims, the Baha'i Faith, and Jews.

According to the 2000 official census, more than 95 per cent of the population of Barbados is considered to be Christian, although persons may not be active in any particular denomination.

The Anglican Church constitutes the largest religious group, with 70,000 members; an estimated 67 percent are active.

The next largest group is the Seventh-day Adventists (SDA), numbering 16,000 members, 10,000 of whom are active.

There are 11,000 Roman Catholics; an estimated 20 percent are active. Pentecostals number 7,000; more than 50 per cent are active. Methodists number 5,000, according to church officials, although many more claimed Methodist affiliation in the previous official census; an estimated 60 percent are active.

There are 2,500 members of Jehovah's Witnesses; more than 95 per cent are active. There are also Baptists,

Moravians, and members of the Church of Jesus Christ of Latter-day Saints (Mormons) in small numbers.

The number of non-Christians n Barbados is small. There are 4,000 Muslims, most of whom are immigrants or descendants of Indian immigrants from the Indian state of Gujarat.

There are three mosques and an Islamic centre.

Other religious groups include Rastafarians, Hindus, Buddhists, and and members of the Baha'i Faith.

Religion in Barbados plays an important role in life on the island. With its long British ties, the Anglican Church serves the largest segment of the population. The Christian population celebrates its deeply-rooted faith in an annual festival, Gospelfest. Smaller Jewish. Hindu, and Muslim communities add some religious diversity.

In addition to Gospelfest, Barbados holds many other carnivals and festivals.

The Landship is a Barbadian tradition. It mimics and parodies the Royal Navy, and incorporates music, dance and games.

The largest and most important festival in Barbados is Crop Over which celebrates the end of the sugarcane harvest. Lasting three weeks, it includes fairs, parades, and contests.

Education

Education in Barbados is fashioned after the British model. The government of Barbados spends roughly 20 per cent of its annual national budget on education.

All young people in the country must attend school until age sixteen. Barbados' literacy rate is ranked close to 100 per cent, with the minister of education stating that Barbados was in the top 5 countries worldwide for literacy rate, thus placing the country alongside many of the industrialised nations of the world.

Barbados has more than 70 primary schools and more

than 20 secondary schools throughout the island. There are also a number of private schools catering to various teaching models including Montessori and International Baccalaureate.

Degree-level education in the country is provided by the Barbados Community College, the Samuel Jackman Prescod Polytechnic, and a local Cave Hill campus of the University of the West Indies (UWI).

In addition, there is one public senior school.

Education is provided free of charge and is compulsory between the ages of 5 and 16. Attendance is strictly enforced.

It has been reported that Barbados has spent roughly US$15 billion on Education since independence in 1966. In 2006 during the inaugural Cecil F. deCaires Memorial Lecture at the Frank Collymore Hall, the former Central Bank Governor Sir Courtney Blackman remarked that between 1966 and 2000, successive Barbadian governments had spent US$15 billion on education – "a remarkable investment for such a small state."

In 2009, Minister of Education and Human Resource Development Ronald Jones said the Barbados government spent $290 million to upgrade schools by providing information technology.

Culture

The culture of Barbados is a blend of West African and British cultures. The Bajan, or Barbadian dialect, is an iconic part of the culture. But English is dominant in official circles, reflecting centuries of British rule.

British Influence

The island's British influence stretches back to 1625 when Captain John Powell claimed it in the name of King

James I. The first colonists arrived two years later, founding a settlement of 80 civilians and 10 slaves.

Early on, Barbados adopted the British form of government, creating a parliamentary democracy in 1639. During the colonial period, all members of the Legislative Assembly were white.

After slavery was abolished in 1838, non-whites quickly began to play a role in the island's government, with the first minority member elected in 1843.

Although Barbados gained full independence from Britain in 1966, it has retained the governmental style of the former colonial power and many elements of British culture. And probably more than any other former British colony in the region, Barbados stands out as a prominent outpost of Anglo-Saxon culture and traditions.

In addition to the British form of government which is an integral part of the island's national identity, British sports also constitute a very important part of this identity. Cricket is the best example.

The British passed down their love of cricket. It has become a national sport and is the most popular game in Barbados.

The island's cricket team has won numerous regional matches. Many Barbadian players have distinguished themselves on the West Indian team and have competed in international games. One of the most highly regarded cricket players of all time, Sir Garfield Sobers, is a native of Barbados.

The country's architecture is another highly significant feature of British influence and cultural landscape on the island, with many historic buildings still standing. Some were built centuries ago.

In addition to traditional wood and stone, coral was also used in construction, lending a unique Barbadian flair. Jacobean, Georgian, and Victorian styles dominate.

But it was slaves who constructed many of these buildings as well as their own chattel houses. Therefore they are an integral part of the island's architectural legacy.

Built of wood, chattel houses were set atop blocks instead of permanent foundations so they could be easily moved from place to place. The vivid colours of these chattel houses clearly show West African influence.

Music

Music is an important part of the island's culture. Modern Barbados has produced many popular stars of calypso and the indigenous sponge style. The island also has a large jazz scene. Reggae, soca, and tuk are popular as well.

Every January, Barbados hosts the Barbados Jazz Festival. In mid-February, Barbados hosts the Barbados Holetown Festival which celebrates the arrival of the first English settlers.

The music of Barbados includes distinctive national styles of folk and popular music including elements of Western classical and religious music.

The culture of Barbados is a syncretic mix of African and British elements, and the island's music reflects this mix through song styles and types, instrumentation, dances, and aesthetic principles.

Barbadian folk traditions – in addition to the Landship movement which is a satirical, informal organisation based on the British Navy – includes tea meetings, tuk bands and numerous traditional songs and dances.

Most of the popular styles of music have been imported from Trinidad and Tobago, the United States and elsewhere.

And along with Trinidad, Cuba, Puerto Rico, and the Virgin Islands, Barbados is one of the few centres for Caribbean jazz.

Characteristics and musical identity

In addition to being a mixture of African and British forms of music, Barbadian musical culture also has unique elements that may traced to indigenous sources including Amerindian.

There has also been culture conflict in the Barbadian context; a phenomenon that has also been observed in other Caribbean island nations.

The conflict has taken place through the centuries between Anglo-Saxon and African cultures because the latter are considered to be inferior even by some Afro-Caribbeans including those in the diaspora.

In Barbados, tension between African and British culture has long been a major element of Barbadian history, and has included the banning of certain African-derived practices and black Barbadian parodies of British traditions.

Simple entertainment is the basis for most Barbadians' participation in music and dance activities, though religious and other functional musics also occur.

Barbadian folk culture declined in importance in the 20th century but rekindled in the 1970s when many Barbadians became interested in their national culture and history. This change was heralded by the arrival of spouge, a popular national genre that reflects Barbadian heritage and African origins.

Spouge helped kindle a resurgence in national pride and came to be viewed as Barbados' answer to the popular Caribbean genres of reggae and calypso from Jamaica and Trinidad, respectively.

The religious music of the Barbadian Christian churches plays an important role in Barbadian musical identity, especially in urban areas.

Many distinctive Barbadian musical and other cultural

traditions are derived from parodies of Anglican church hymns and British military drills. The British military performed drills to both provide security for the island's population and intimidate slaves.

Modern Barbadian tea meetings, tuk bands, the Landship tradition and many folk songs come from slaves parodying the practices of white authorities.

British-Barbadians used music for cultural and intellectual enrichment and to feel a sense of kinship and connection with the British Isles through the maintenance of British musical forms.

Plantation houses featured music as entertainment at balls, dances and other gatherings.

For Afro-Barbadians, drum, vocal and dance music was an integral part of everyday life, and songs and performance practices were created for normal, everyday events and special celebrations such as Whitsuntide, Christmas, Easter, Landship and Crop Over. These songs remain an integral part of Barbadian culture and form a rich folk repertoire.

Western classical music is the most socially accepted form of musical expression for Barbadians in Bridgetown, including a variety of vocal music, chamber and orchestral music, and piano and violin.

Along with hymns, oratorios, cantatas and other religious music, chamber music of the Western tradition remains an important part of Barbadian musical through an integral role in the services of the Anglican church.

History of music in Barbados

The music of Barbados draws on the island's cultural heritage. It also reflects the island's diverse cultures and history.

When slavery was going on between 1627- and 1838, African music was common among the slaves. It included work songs, funeral and religious music. Although slave owners initially allowed dances, this ended in 1688 out of fear that the slaves might plan a rebellion at such festivities. The same law, passed in 1630, also prohibited the use of drums and horns which were feared might be used as a form of communication to facilitate slave rebellions.

The elite plantocracy of the island during the colonial era also felt that Christianity was ill-suited for slaves; instead, the Church of England sent missionaries to convert slaves to Christianity.

Any cultural element of apparent African origin was suppressed in the name of promoting Christianity. Legal restrictions furthered this goal by banning parties on Sundays, the Christian day of rest, as well as dances like the outdoors fertility dance, *Jean and Johnnie*.

But, in spite of legal restrictions, traditional African music continued. This included the use of drums and rattles, and declamatory and improvised call and response vocals.

A lot of African music was used in *obeah*, an African religion found throughout the island.

By the beginning of the 19th century, slaves provided most of the musical accompaniment for plantation festivities such as the Harvest Home, while the white elites participated in dignity balls.

With the slave population approaching three times the white population, many slave owners feared revolts. This led to the Slave Consolidation Act in 1826 which reaffirmed the ban on drums and horns.

Christian missionaries also discouraged the performance of African music. But this restriction only pushed the music underground where it was passed through secret societies and rituals.

Slavery in Barbados was finally ended in 1838 and newly-emancipated blacks celebrated with instruments including drums and horns, as well as banjos, tambourines and xylophones. However, the use of horns and drums was still discouraged, leading to the primacy of vocal music; at the same time, new Protestant churches from North America moved into the island, bringing with them American parlor music, cowboy songs and revivalist hymns.

Following emancipation, ensembles consisting of snare and bass drums, flute and triangle emerged; these were called tuk bands, and may have been based on British fife-and-drum corps.

They used African polyrhythms and syncopation and accompanied the community dance troupe Landship which simulated the movement of ships at sea through dance. They also used them at various kinds of celebrations and festivals.

In 1889, the Royal Barbados Police Band was formed. This instrumental ensemble remains popular and has performed across the world. It has counterparts in other former British colonies not only in the Caribbean but also in Africa and elsewhere; one good example being the Tanzania Police Band which was famous in the sixties and seventies and won international competitions during that period under the leadership of its renowned conductor Mayagila.

Calypso music arrived in Barbados from Trinidad in the first part of the 20th century. It did not have many fans in Barbados during those years and only a few Barbadian calypsonians emerged on the scene. They included Da Costa Allamby and Mighty Charmer.

Beginning in the 1940s when the Crop Over festival was cancelled due to the decline of the sugarcane industry, Barbados has seen the influx of popular music from other countries, including the United States, United Kingdom, Jamaica and Cuba.

Following independence in 1966, Barbadian calypso became more popular, especially The Merrymen band which is known for such songs as "Brudda Neddy" and

"Millie Gone to Brazil." Jackie Opel, a Barbadian singer, also came on the scene playing a blend of calypso and reggae that evolved into spouge music.

Spouge was immensely popular in Barbados from about 1969 to 1973.

In 1974, the Crop Over festival was revived, featuring calypso competitions; as a result, calypso's popularity grew rapidly, overshadowing spouge and other genres, with only dub music achieving equal stature.

Although the island was inhabited before the 1500s, little is known about Barbadian music before the arrival of the Portuguese in 1536 and then the English in 1627.

The Portuguese left little influence but English culture and music helped shape the island's heritage.

Irish and Scottish settlers immigrated to the island in the 1600s to work in the tobacco industry. They brought with them more new music, in addition to what was already there from Britain and Africa.

The middle of the 1700s saw the decline of the tobacco industry and the rise of sugarcane as well as the introduction of large numbers of African slaves.

Brazilian exiles however, along with sugarcane, introduced Samba to the island which featured a mixture of Latin music with African influences. It soon developed into Soca-Samba which is indigenous to Barbados.

Modern Barbadian music is thus largely a combination of English and African elements, with Irish, Scottish, and modern American and Caribbean – especially Jamaican – influences.

By the 19th century, the Barbadian colonialists grew to fear slave revolts, and specifically, the use of music as a tool of communication and planning for revolution. As a result, the government passed laws to restrict musical activities among slaves.

At the same time, American and other forms of imported music were brought to Barbados, while many important elements of modern Barbadian music, like tuk bands, also emerged. And in the 20th century, many new styles were imported into the island, the most influential being reggae, calypso, soca, ska, and jazz. Barbados became home to many performers of these new genres, especially soca and calypso, while the island also produced an indigenous style called spouge which became an important symbol of Barbadian identity.

Folk music

Barbadian culture and music are mixtures of European and African elements, with minimal influence from the indigenous peoples of the island, about whom little is known.

Significant numbers of Asian, specifically Chinese and Japanese, people have moved to Barbados, but their music is unstudied and has had little impact on Barbadian music.

The earliest reference to Afro-Barbadian music may come from a description of a slave rebellion, in which the rebels were inspired to fight by music played on skin drums, conch trumpets and animal horns.

Slavery continued, however, and the colonial and slave-owning authorities eventually outlawed musical instruments among slaves.

By the end of the 1600s, a distinctly Barbadian folk culture developed based on influences and instruments from Africa, Britain and other Caribbean islands.

Early Barbadian folk music was a major part of life among the island's slave population. Even severe legal restrictions and other harsh measures against the slaves failed to suffocate that.

For the slaves, music was "essential for recreation and dancing and as a part of the life cycle for communication and religious meaning."

African musicians also provided the music for the white landowners' private parties; while the slaves developed their own party music, culminating in the Crop

Over festival which began in 1688.

The earliest crop over festivals featured dancing and call-response.; a call-response style is typical African style. Singing was accompanied by *shak-shak*, banjo, bones and bottles containing varying amounts of water.

Song

Barbadian folk songs are heavily influenced by the music of England. Many traditional songs concern events current at the time of their composition; for example, the emancipation of slaves in Barbados; and the coronations of Queen Victoria, King George V, and Queen Elizabeth II. This song tradition dates back to 1650.

The most influential Barbadian folk songs are associated with the island's lower-class labourers who have held on to their folk heritage.

Some Barbadian songs and stories made their way back to England, most famously "Inckle the English Sailor" and "Yarico the Indian Maid" which became English plays and an opera by George Coleman with music by Samuel Arnold and first performed in London in 1787.

Dance

Barbadian folk dances include a wide variety of styles performed at Lanship, holidays and other occasions. Dancers and other performers at the crop over festivals, for example, are popular and an iconic part of Barbadian culture, known for dancing in the costumes of sugarcane-cutters.

The Landship movement features song and dance meant to imitate the passage of a British navy ship through rough seas; Landship and other occasions also feature African-derived improvised and complexly-rhythmic dances, and British hornpipes, jigs, maypole dances and marches.

The Jean and Johnnie dance was an important part of Barbadian culture until it was banned in the 19th century. This was a popular fertility dance performed outdoors at plantation fairs and other festivals and was functional in that it allowed women to show off to men and, more rarely, vice versa. The dance was eventually banned because it was associated with non-Christian African traditions.

Instrumentation

The Barbadian folk tradition is home to a great variety of musical instruments imported from Africa, Great Britain or other Caribbean islands.

The most central instrument group in Barbadian culture is the percussion instruments. These include numerous drums, among them the *pump* and the *tum-tum*, made from a hollowed-out tree trunk; the side snare drum and a double-headed bass drum of tuk bands.

Folk musicians also use gongs made from tree trunks, bones, rock jaw, triangle, cynbals, bottles filled with water, and xylophones.

Rattles are also widespread and include the pan-Antillean *shak-shak* and the calabash, *de shot and rattle*. More recently, imported folk percussion instruments include the conga and bongo from Puerto Rico, the Dominican Republic and Cuba but whose origin is Africa, and the tambourine.

String and wind instruments also play an important role in Barbadian folk culture, especially the bow-fiddle, banjo and acoustic guitar; more modern groups also use an electric and bass guitar.

The *shukster* is a distinctive instrument made by stretching a guitar string between two sides of a house.

Traditional Barbadian wind instruments are largely metal, but in their folk origins, were made out of locally found materials. Barbadian villagers burned finger holes, for example, on bamboo tubes, made trumpets out of conch shells and pipes from pumpkin vines.

Many modern groups use harmonica, accordion, alto and tenor saxophone, trumpet, and trombone.

Religious music

Although Western classical and other musics play an important role in Anglican church services on Barbados, religion and folk music are closely intertwined in everyday lives of most Barbadians.

The basis for religious folk music is the Anglican hymn, a kind of praise song mostly sung on Sundays, a day when Christian Barbadians come together with family members to sing and praise God to ask for strength for the next week's work.

Pentecostal music has become a part of Barbadian religious and musical traditions since the 1920s. Music plays an important role in Pentecostal ceremonies and is provided by emotional and improvised performances accompanied by tambourines.

In addition to the Anglican and Pentecostal traditions, Rastafarian music has spread to Barbados in more recent years, along with African American musical forms, especially gospel, and the Spiritual Baptist religion which is derived from the Trinidadian Shango cult that spread to Barbados in the 1960s.

One of the more internationally known religious music groups from Barbados are the The Silvetones of Barbados.

Holidays, festivals and other celebrations

A number of holidays, festivals and other celebrations play an integral role in Barbadian folk, and popular, music. Whitsuntide, Christmas, Easter are important, each associated with their own musical traditions, as are distinctly Barbadian festivities like the Crop Over Festival and the Landship movement.

The original crop over festival celebrated the end of the sugarcane harvest. These festivals were held in the great house of the plantations and included both slaves and plantation managers.

Celebrations included drinking competitions, feasting, song and dance, and climbing a greased pole. Musical accompaniment was provided by triangle, fiddle, drums and a guitar, played by slave entertainers.

Crop over festivals continue to play an important part in Barbadian culture and always feature music by performers in sugarcane-cutting costumes, even though many modern performers are not themselves sugarcane-cutters.

The Barbadian Landship movement, an informal entertainment organisation which mocks – through mimicry and satire – the British navy, began in 1837. It was started by an individual variously known as *Moses Ward* and *Moses Wood*, in Britton's Hall in Seamen's Village.

The structure of the Landship organisation mirrors the structure of the British navy, with a "ship" which is connected to a "dock" – a wooden house similar to a chattel house – and leaders known as *Lord High Admiral*, *Captain*, *Boatswain* and other navy ranks.

Each unit is named like a typical navy ship and may include actual names of British ships or places.

Landship performances symbolise and reflect the passage of ships through rough seas. Parades, jigs, hornpipes, maypole dances and other music and dance types are a part of the Landship Society's celebrations. The Council of the Barbados Landship Association regulates the movement.

Barbadian Christmas music is mostly based on church and concert hall performances where typical North

American Christmas carols are performed – such as "White Christmas" and "Silver Bells," alongside works by English composers like William Byrd, Henry Walford Davies and Thomas Tallis.

In more recent years, calypso, reggae and other new elements have become a major part of local Christmas traditions.

As recently as the 1960s, Barbados was home to a distinctive practice in which *scrubbers* travelled from house to house singing hymns and receiving rewards from households.

Tuk bands and tea meetings

Tuk bands are Barbadian musical ensembles, consisting of a bow-fiddle or pennywhistle flute, kittle triangle and a snare and double-headed bass drum. The kittle and bass drum provide the rhythm, while the flute gives the melody.

The drums are light-weight. So they can be carried easily. They're made by both rural villagers and drummers using cured sheepskin and goatskin.

Tuk bands are based on the British military's regimental bands which played for many years for special occasions like visiting royalty and coronations.

The tuk sound has evolved through the years, as has the instrumentation, with the bow-fiddle used before being most commonly replaced by the pennywhistle flute.

Tuk bands are now most common in Landship events. But they're still independently functional without always being a part of Landship performances.

On their own, tuk bands are generally accompanied by a range of iconic Barbadian characters, including "shaggy bears," "mother sally," "the steel donkey" and "green monkeys."

The upbeat modern sound of tuk ensembles are a

distinctly Barbadian blend of African and British musics.

Tea meetings are celebrations held in society lodges or school halls and feature both solo and group performance, theatrical rhetoric and oratory and other activities. After declining following World War 1, tea meetings have recently been revived and have regained their widespread popularity. They are held at night, beginning at 9:00 PM and continue until midnight when there is a two-hour break for food and drink before the tea meeting is resumed.

Popular music

Barbados has produced few internationally popular musicians, worldwide pop superstar Rihanna being the most famous. It has, however, a well-developed local scene for imported styles such as American jazz and calypso as well as the indigenous spouge style.

Calypso was the first popular music in Barbados and dates back to the 1930s.

Barbadian calypso is a comedic song form accompanied by guitar and banjo. More recent styles of calypso have also kept the local scene alive and have produced a number of famous calypsonians.

Spouge is a mixture of calypso and other styles, especially ska, and became very popular in the 1960s around the same time that the Barbadian jazz scene grew in stature and became home to a number of famous performers.

Modern Barbadian popular music is largely based on reggae, ragga and socca, and includes some elements of indigenous styles.

Artists like Terencia Coward have used modern popular music with instrumentation borrowed from folk tuk bands.

Two of the more well-known bands of Barbadian

popular music are Krosfyah and Square One (now defunct). The new wave of singers, largely soca, include Rupee, Lil' Rick and Jabae with lead vocalist Bruce and Barry Chandler, all recent winners at Crop Over.

Calypso

Before the 1930s, Barbadian calypso was called *banja* and was performed by labourers in village-tenantry areas. Itinerant minstrels like Mighty Jerry, Shilling Agard and Slammer were well-known forerunners of modern Barbadian calypso. Their song tradition embraced sentimentality, humour and opinionated lyrics which continued to the 1960s, often by then accompanied by guitar or banjo.

The mid-1900s brought new forms of music from Trinidad, Brazil, the United States, Cuba and the Dominican Republic to Barbados, and the Barbadian calypso style came to be viewed as lowbrow or inferior.

However, promoters like Lord Silvers and Mighty Dragon kept the popular tradition alive through shows at the Globe Theatre, featuring pioneers Mighty Romeo, Sir Don Marshall, Lord Radio and the Bimshire Boys and Mike Wilkinson. These performers set the stage for the development of popular Barbadian calypso in the 1960s.

In the early 1960s, Barbadian calypso grew in popularity and stature, led by Viper, Mighty Gabby and The Merrymen.

The first calypso competitions were held in 1960, and they quickly grew larger and more prominent.

The Merrymen became the island's most prominent contribution to calypso by the 1970s and into the 80s. Their style, known as *blue beat*, incorporated Barbadian folk songs and ballads as well as American blues, country music and a distinctive sound created by harmonica, guitar and banjo.

By the beginning of the 1980s, *kaiso*, a form of stage-presented calypso pioneered in Trinidad, was widespread at Crop Over and other celebrations.

In 1984, the National Cultural Foundation helped to promote and administer calypso festivals which attracted tourists, stimulating the calypso industry.

As a result, calypso has become a very visible and iconic part of Barbadian culture, and some calypsonians have become internationally renowned. They include Mighty Gabby and Red Plastic Bag.

Spouge

Spouge is a style of Barbadian popular music created by Jackie Opel in the 1960s. It's primarily a fusion of Jamaican ska with Trinidadian calypso. But it's also influenced by a wide variety of music from the British Isles and United States, include sea shanties, hymns and spirituals.

Spouge instrumentation originally consisted of cowbell, bass guitar, trap set and various other electronic and percussion instruments, later augmented by saxophone, trombone and trumpets. Of these, the cowbell and the guitar are widely seen as the most integral part of the instrumentation and are said to reflect the African origin of much of Barbadian music.

Two different kinds of spouge were popular in the 1960s: *raw spouge* (*Draytons Two style*) and *dragon spouge* (*Cassius Clay style*).

The spouge industry grew immensely by the end of the 1970s and produced popular stars such as Blue Rhythm Comb, the Draytons Two and The Troubadours.

Recent years has seen a resurgence of interest in spouge among some quarters, with people like Desmond Weekes of the Draytons Two indicating that spouge should be encouraged because it's a national form of music which can reach international audiences and inspire the nation's pride in its cultural heritage.

Jazz

Jazz is a genre of music from the United States which reached Barbados by the end of the 1920s.

The first major performer from the island was Lionel Gittens who was followed by Percy Green, Maggie Goodridge, and Clevie Gittens. They played a variety of music including swing, a kind of pop-jazz, Barbadian calypso and waltzes.

With little recorded music on the island, radio broadcasts such as Willis Conover's *Voice of America* had a major influence on many people in Barbados.

In 1937, riots over poverty and disenfranchisement erupted, and people like Clement Payne rose to fame advocating reform. In the same year, Payne was deported and riots broke out in Bridgetown, spreading throughout the island.

The following year, the Barbados Labour Party was formed by C. A. Braithwaite and Grantley Adams.

As political awareness among the black majority on the island spread, so did bebop, a kind of jazz which was associated with social activism and Afrocentrism in the United States.

The first Barbadian bebop musician from the island was Keith Campbell, a pianist who had learned to play many styles while living in Trinidad during a time when American soldiers were stationed there, providing a ready market for bands that could play American music.

Other musicians of that period included Ernie Small, a trumpeter and pianist, and band leader St. Clare Jackman.

In the 1950s, rhythm and blues (R&B) and rock-and-roll became popular on the island, and many jazz bands found themselves pushed aside.

A wave of Guyanese musicians also appeared in Barbados. They included Colin Dvall, a saxophonist who later joined the Police Band, and the Ebe Gilkes Quartet.

Although mainstream audiences were still listening to R&B and rock, modern jazz retained a small core of followers into the 1960s. The foundation of the Belair Jazz Club in Bridgetown in 1961 helped to keep the scene alive.

With independence in 1966 came a focus on black Barbadian culture including music such as calypso, reggae and spouge, instead of being preoccupied with British forms of music and standards of musical development. It was also during this period that calypso jazz evolved, pioneered by groups such as Schofield Pilgrim.

This genre of music had developed by 1965 when original works such as "Jouvert Morning" and "Calypso Lament" were composed. Artists including the pianist Adrian Clarke became popular during the '60s as well.

In the early 1970s, jazz fan and critic Carl Moore launched a project to keep jazz alive on the island, while Zanda Alexander's performance in Bridgetown in 1972 is said to be the first Caribbean jazz festival.

Oscar Peterson's 1976 performance in Trinidad also inspired Barbadian musicians, as did the radio programme, *Jazz Jam*, which was broadcast starting in the mid-70s on the Caribbean Broadcasting Corporation (CBC).

However, in 1983, the Belair Jazz Club closed and was not replaced by any long-term clubs.

Later in the 1980s, jazz declined greatly in popularity, although saxophonist Arturo Tappin organised the International Barbados/Caribbean Jazz Festival, while other performances were organised by a group called Friends of Jazz.

More jazz calypso fusion musicians appeared on the scene during this period, including Janice Robertson and her Trinidadian husband Raf.

Music institutions and festivals

The main music festival in Barbados is Crop Over which is celebrated with song, dance, calypso tent competitions and parades, especially leading up to the first Monday in August, what is known as *Kadooment Day*.

Celebrating the end of the sugarcane harvest, the crop festival is inaugurated by the ritual delivery of the last of the harvest on a cart pulled by mules. The sugarcane workers who become champions are crowned King and Queen for the event.

In addition to crop over, music plays an important role in many other Barbadian holidays and festivals. The Easter Oistins Fish Festival, for example, features a street party with music to celebrate the signing of the *Charter of Barbados* and the fishing industry of the island; and the Holetown Festival commemorates the arrival of the first English settlers in Barbados in 1627.

Opera, cabaret and sports are a major part of the Easter holiday season.

On November 30, Independence Day, military bands in parades play marches, calypsos and other popular songs. This is preceded – for several weeks – by the National Independence Festival of Creative Arts.

The National Independence Festival of Creative Arts and Crop Over are two of the festivals sponsored by the National Cultural Foundation (NCF); the other is Congaline, a recently-organised street party that begins in April and ends on May Day. NCF also assists with the Holers Opera Season, Oistins Fish Festival, Holetown Festival and the B'dos Jazz Festival.

Other major musical institutions in Barbados include the Barbados Chamber Orchestra and the Cavite Choral. There are also dance and ballet groups known as Dance National Afrique, Barbados Dance Theatre Company,

Dance Strides, Liz Mahon Dances, Dance Place and Dancing Africa.

The island's music industry is home to several recording studios, the largest being *Blue Wave*, a 48-track system, and *Paradise Alley*, a 24-track system. Others include Chambers' Studio, Gray Lizard Productions and Ocean Lab Studios.

Chapter Five:

British Virgin Islands

THE British Virgin Islands (BVI), also called the Virgin Islands, is a British overseas territory located in the Caribbean the east of Puerto Rico.

The islands are a part of the Virgin Islands archipelago. The remaining islands in the archipelago constitute the U.S. Virgin Islands.

Technically, the official name of the British territory is simply the "Virgin Islands." But in practice since 1917, they have been almost universally referred to as the "British Virgin Islands" to distinguish the from the American Virgin Islands.

The British Virgin Islands consist of the main islands of Tortola, Virgin Gorda, Anegada, and Jost Van Dyke, along with more than 50 other smaller islands and cays. Approximately 15 of the islands are inhabited.

The capital, Road Town, is on Tortola, the largest island. It's approximately 12 miles long and 3 miles wide. The islands have a total population of about 22,000. About 18,000 of them live on Tortola.

History

The Virgin Islands were first settled by the Arawak from South America. They inhabited the islands until the 1400s when they were displaced by the more aggressive Caribs, a tribe from the Lesser Antilles islands. The Caribbean Sea is named after the Caribs; so is the region which is simply known as the Caribbean.

The first European to see the Virgin Islands was Christopher Columbus in 1493 on his second voyage to the Americas.

The Spaniards claimed the islands in the early 1500s but never settled there. Subsequent years saw the English, Dutch, French, Spanish and Danish jostling for control of the region which became a notorious for piracy.

There is no record of any native Amerindian population in the British Virgin Islands during this period, although the native population on nearby St. Croix was decimated. Some Carib Amerindians still live on nearby St. Croix.

The Dutch established a permanent settlement on the island of Tortola by 1648.

In 1672, the English captured Tortola from the Dutch. And in 1680, the annexed Anegada and Virgin Gorda. The Danish gained control of the nearby islands of St. Thomas, St. John and St. Croix between 1672 and 1733.

The British islands were mainly considered to be a strategic possession. But they were also used to grow crops when conditions were favourable.

The British introduced sugarcane and brought slaves from Africa to work on the plantations. Sugarcane became the main crop and source of foreign trade.

The islands prospered until the middle of the 1800s when a combination of factors – the abolition of slavery, a series of disastrous hurricanes, and increased production of sugar beet in Europe and in the United States – significantly reduced sugarcane production and led to a period of economic decline.

In 1917, the United States purchased St. John, St. Thomas and St. Croix from Denmark for US$25 million, renaming them the United States Virgin Islands.

The British Virgin Islands were, at different times, administered as part of the British Leeward Islands or with St. Kitts and Nevis. An Administrator represented the British government on the islands.

The islands gained colonial status in 1960 and became autonomous in 1967.

Since the 1960s, the islands have diversified their economy and have moved away from predominantly agricultural production to tourism and financial services, becoming one of the wealthiest areas in the Caribbean.

Geography

The British Virgin Islands comprise about 60 tropical Caribbean islands ranging in size from the largest – Tortola island – to tiny uninhabited islets. The islands are only a few miles east of the U.S. Virgin Islands.

The North Atlantic Ocean lies to the north of the islands, and the Caribbean Sea lies to the south.

Most of the islands are volcanic in origin and have a hilly, rugged terrain.

Anegada is geologically distinct from the rest of the group and is a flat island composed of limestone and coral.

Climate

The British Virgin Islands enjoy a tropical climate moderated by trade winds.

Temperatures vary little throughout the year. In the capital, Road Town, typical maximum temperature is around 89.6°F in the summer and 84.2°F in the winter. And typical daily minimum temperature is 75.2°F in the summer and 69.8°F in the winter.

Rainfall is higher in the hills and lower on the coast. It can be quite variable but the wettest months on average are September to November and the driest months on average are February and March.

Hurricanes occasionally hit the islands. The hurricane season runs from June to November.

Politics

Politics of the British Virgin Islands takes place in a framework of a parliamentary representative democratic dependency whereby the premier is the head of government under a multi-party system.

The British Virgin Islands are an internally self-governing overseas territory of the United Kingdom.

The United Nations Committee on Decolonization includes the islands on the United Nations list of Non-Self-Governing Territories.

Executive power is exercised by the government. Legislative power is vested in both the government and the Legislative Council.

The Judiciary is independent of the executive and the legislature.

Executive authority in the British Virgin Islands is invested in The Queen and is exercised on her behalf by the governor of the British Virgin Islands.

The governor, a resident of the British Virgin Islands, is appointed by the Queen on the advice of the British government.

Defence and Foreign Affairs remain the responsibility of the United Kingdom.

Economy

The British Virgin Islands is one of the most prosperous parts of the Caribbean. According to the *CIA World Factbook* in 2004, the territory had the 12th highest GDP per capita in the world. It had a per capita GDP of around $38,500 in 2004.

The economy is fuelled by financial services which generate about 52 per cent of government revenues; and by tourism which accounts for nearly all of the rest. The economy also benefits from the territory's status as a tax haven.

Government's revenue comes directly from licence fees for offshore companies. And considerable further sums are raised directly or indirectly from payroll taxes relating to salaries paid within the trust industry sector; these salaries which tend to be higher on average than those paid in the tourism sector.

But tourism employs more people than the financial services sector does. And a larger proportion of the businesses in the tourist industry are locally owned. Also, a large number of highly tourism-dependent sole traders such as taxi drivers and street vendors are local people.

Tourism accounts for 45 per cent of national income. The islands are a popular destination for American citizens.

In 2006, 825,603 people visited the islands – of whom 443,987 were cruise ship passengers.

Tourists frequent the numerous white sand beaches, visit The Baths on Virgin Gorda, snorkel the coral reefs near Anegada, or experience the well-known bars of Jost Van Dyke.

The British Virgin Islands (BVI) are known as one of the world's greatest sailing destinations, and charter sailboats are a very popular way to visit less accessible islands.

Every year since 1972, the BVI has hosted the Spring Regatta which is a seven-day collection of sailing races throughout the islands.

A substantial number of the tourists who visit the BVI are cruise ship passengers, although they produce far lower revenue per head than charter-boat tourists and hotel-based tourists. They're, nonetheless, important to the substantial – and politically important – taxi driving community.

Substantial revenues are also generated by the registration of offshore companies. As of June 2008, 823,502 companies were registered – of which 445,865 were active.

In 2000, KPMG reported in its survey of offshore jurisdictions for the United Kingdom government that more than 41 per cent of the world's offshore companies were formed in the British Virgin Islands.

Since 2001, financial services in the British Virgin Islands have been regulated by the independent Financial Services Commission.

While at one time the BVI was well regarded as a good domicile for captive insurance services, this changed in recent years with the change of insurance regulators in 2007 and the government's increasing pressure to hire only locals in the insurance industry.

Local people are known as – and call themselves – "belongers" to distinguish themselves from outsiders or from those who don't "belong" there.

It's a term used in other Caribbean islands by those who claim native or indigenous status – in terms of birthright – hence more rights as opposed to foreigners even if the foreigners have legal status and the right to live there. It's also a term that generates and fuels nationalist sentiments sometimes in a militant form in terms of rhetoric. In its extreme form, the attitude of some "belongers" is: "We belong here; you don't."

Agriculture and industry account for only a small percentage of the British Virgin Islands' gross domestic product. Agricultural products includes fruit, vegetables, sugarcane, livestock and poultry. Industries include rum distillation, construction and boat building.

Since 1959, the official currency of the British Virgin Islands (BVI) has been the American dollar which is also used by the United States Virgin Islands. The BVI chose to use the American dollar because of traditionally close links with the U.S. Virgin Islands and because of the strength of the currency.

The British Virgin Islands are a major target for drug traffickers who use the area as a gateway to the United States. According to the Foreign & Commonwealth Office, "Problems associated with drug trafficking are potentially the most serious threat to stability in the BVI."

Tourism

An estimated 350,000 tourists, mainly from the United States visited the islands in 1997; and more than 800,000 in 2006.

The bulk of the tourism income in the British Virgin Islands is generated by the yacht chartering industry.

The territory has relatively few large hotels compared to other tourism centres in the Caribbean.

Financial services

In the mid-1980s, the government began offering offshore registration to companies wishing to incorporate in the islands, and incorporation fees now generate substantial revenues.

An estimated 550,000 companies were on the offshore registry by the end of 2004.

The adoption of a comprehensive insurance law in late

1994, which provides a blanket of confidentiality with regulated statutory gateways for investigation of criminal offences, is expected to make the British Virgin Islands even more attractive to international business.

The British Virgin Islands is one of the world's leading offshore financial centres. About 42 per cent of the estimated 1.1 million offshore companies incorporated worldwide are registered in the British Virgin Islands, making the BVI virtually the world's capital of offshore companies.

Former president of the BVI's Financial Services Commission, Michael Riegels, recites the anecdote that the offshore finance industry commenced on an unknown date in the 1970s when a lawyer from a firm in New York telephoned him with a proposal to incorporate a company in the British Virgin Islands to take advantage of a double taxation relief treaty with the United States. Within a few years, hundreds of such companies had been incorporated in the British Virgin Islands.

This eventually came to the attention of the United States government which unilaterally revoked the treaty in 1981.

In 1984 the British Virgin Islands, trying to recapture some of the lost offshore business, enacted a new form of companies legislation, the International Business Companies Act, under which an offshore company which was exempt from local taxes could be formed.

This had only limited success until 1991 when the United States invaded Panama to oust General Manuel Noriega. At the time, Panama was one of the largest providers of offshore financial services in the world. But the offshore financial service operators fled Panama because of the invasion and the British Virgin Islands was one of the main beneficiaries.

And on 12 April 2007, the London *Financial Times* reported that the British Virgin Islands was the second largest source of foreign direct investment (FDI) in the world surpassed only by Hong Kong. Almost all of this capital is attributable to investment through the BVI's offshore finance industry.

Agriculture

The livestock sector is the most important sector in agriculture. Farming is limited because of poor soils which limit the islands' ability to produce enough food for local consumption.

Demographics

The population of the British Virgin Islands is about 30,000.

The majority of the population – about 83 per cent – are Afro-Caribbean descended from African slaves brought to the islands by the British.

Other large ethnic groups include those of British origin. They constitute the largest segment of the white community in the British Virgin Islands. Whites constitute about 7 per cent of the BVI's population.

The islands are heavily dependent on migrant labour. In 2004, migrant workers constituted 50 per cent of the total population.

About 32 per cent of all workers employed in the British Virgin Islands work for the government.

Transport

There is a road network of 70 miles.

The main airport – Terrance B. Lettsome International Airport which is also known as Beef Island Airport – is located on Beef Island which lies off the eastern tip of Tortola Island and is accessible by the Queen Elizabeth II Bridge.

Virgin Gorda and Anegada islands have their own smaller airports.

The main harbour is in the capital Road Town. There are also ferries that operate within the British Virgin Islands and to the neighbouring United States Virgin Islands.

As in the United kingdom, cars in the British Virgin Islands drive on the left side of the road.

The roads are often quite steep and winding, and ruts can be a problem when it rains.

Education

The British Virgin Islands operates several government schools as well as private schools. There is also a community college, H. Lavity Stoutt Community College, which is located at the eastern end of Tortola.

Sports

Because of its location and climate, the British Virgin Islands has long been a haven for sailing enthusiasts. Sailing is regarded as one of the foremost sports in all of the BVI.

Calm waters along with steady breezes provide some of the best sailing conditions not only in the Caribbean but in the whole world.

There are many sailing events in the British Virgin Islands throughout the year. The largest and most well-known event is a week-long series of sailing races called the Spring Regatta.

This is the premier sailing event of the Caribbean. With several races hosted each day, different kinds of boats are used, from full-size mono-hull yachts to dinghies. Captains and their crews come from many parts of the world to participate in the event.

The Spring Regatta is part race, part party, part festival. There are races, games, and music during the day, and a lot of partying at night.

The Spring Regatta is normally held in the first week of April every year.

Culture

The British Virgin Islands is a blend of cultures representing various peoples who have inhabited the archipelago through the centuries.

Although the territories – British and U.S. Virgin Islands which collectively constitute the archipelago – are politically separate, they maintain close cultural ties.

Like much of the Anglophone Caribbean, the culture of the Virgin Islands – both British and American – is a product of West African, European and American cultural influences.

Although Danish settlers controlled what is now U.S. Virgin Islands for many years, they left very little behind in terms of cultural influence. Instead, the dominant language in the entire archipelago has been an English-based Creole since the 19th century. And the islands remain much more receptive to British culture than any other.

But the Dutch, the French and the Danish also contributed elements to the island's culture, as have immigrants from the Arab world, India and other Caribbean islands.

However, the single largest influence on modern Virgin Island culture comes from Africans who were enslaved to work in the sugarcane fields from the 17th to the mid-19th century.

The slaves brought with them traditions from a wide swathe of Africa, including what is now Nigeria, Senegal, Gambia, Ghana, Congo, and elsewhere including parts of

East Africa, especially what is now Tanzania and Mozambique especially after anti-slavery patrols intensified on the West African coast when the slave trade was abolished, forcing slave traders to turn their attention to East Africa.

The Virgin Islands culture continues to undergo creolisation as a result of inter-Caribbean migration and cultural contact with other parts in the region including the United States.

Migration has changed the social landscape of both parts of the Virgin Islands – British and American – to such an extent that half of the population in the British Virgin Islands is of foreign origin, mostly Caribbean; and in the U.S. Virgin Islands, most native-born residents can trace their ancestry to other Caribbean islands.

Cuisines

Traditional food tends to be spicy and hearty. Much of the foods are imported due to the islands' poor soil quality, little available farmland, and a taste for foreign foods.

Upscale restaurants often cater to tourists, serving a combination of North American dishes with tropical twists as well as local cuisine. An example of this is the addition of mango and Caribbean spices to salmon, a non-tropical fish.

Dishes

Fungi (pronounced fun-gee) is a main staple of the Virgin Islands diet. It consists of cornmeal that has been boiled and cooked to a thick consistency along with okra. Fungi is usually eaten with boiled fish or salt fish.

Callaloo (sometimes spelled kallaloo) is a soup made from callaloo bush/leaf, often substituted with spinach. It consists of various meats and okra, and is boiled to a thick stew consistency.

Because of inter-Caribbean migration, many foods from other Caribbean countries have been incorporated into the Virgin Islands culinary culture. For example, one of the popular dishes is roti, of Indo-Trinidadian origin, which consists of curried vegetables and meat wrapped in a paper-thin dough.

Local Fruits

Fruits eaten in the Virgin Islands include sour apple, mango, papaya, genip, sea grapes, tamarinds which can be made in a sweet stew or rolled in sweet balls; and goose berries which are small green sour fruit, smaller than a grape. They're mainly stewed together with sugar for a sweet snack.

Drinks

Bush tea, maubi and sorrel are some of the drinks from the Virgin Islands.

Snacks

One of the most popular snacks is pate (pronounced PAH-TEH). It's a fried bread with various meats including beef, chicken or salt fish stuffed inside.

Johnny cake, originally known as journey cake, is a popular pastry.

Music of the Virgin Islands

The traditional music of the British Virgin Islands is called *fungi*, named after the local cornmeal dish with the same name.

The special sound of fungi is due to a unique local

fusion between African and European music.

Fungi music also functions as a medium of local history and folklore. It's a cherished cultural form of expression that is part of the curriculum in BVI schools.

The fungi bands, also called "scratch bands," use instruments ranging from calabash, washboard, bongos, and ukulele to more traditional Western instruments such as keyboard, banjo, guitar, bass, triangle and saxophone.

Apart from being a form of festive dance music, fungi often contains humorous social commentaries as well as BVI oral history.

The popular singer Iyaz is from the British Virgin Islands.

The music of the Virgin Islands also reflects long-standing cultural ties to the island nations to the south as well as to various European colonialists. From its neighbours, the Virgin Islands have imported various pan-Caribbean genres of music including calypso from Trinidad and reggae from Jamaica.

The major indigenous form of music is the scratch band music – also called *fungi band* music in the British Virgin Islands – which uses improvised instruments like gourds and washboards to produce a kind of music called *quelbe*.

A Virgin Island folk song called *cariso* is also popular; so is St. Thomas' *bamboula*.

The quadrille is the traditional folk dance of the islands performed by groups such as St. Croix's Imperial Quadrille and St. Thomas' Flat German Quadrille.

It was formerly an important part of Virgin Islands culture; it's now rarely performed except on St. Croix where locals dance the quadrille at public performance venues such as St. Gerard's Hall or as educational spectacles for schools, festivals and holidays, or as entertainment for tourists.

Educational and entertainment quadrille troops both wear traditionally styled clothing reminiscent of authentic attire.

The Heritage Dancers are a respected dance troupe that performs traditional folk dances from the Virgin Islands and beyond.

Folk music

Virgin Island folk music has declined since the mid-20th century, although some traditional groups such as scratch bands remain vibrant.

Factors which contributed to the decline include the rise of the tourism industry which has brought foreign influences, including foreign music, into the islands; the switch of American tourists from Cuba to the Virgin Islands – following the 1959 revolution which swept Castro into power – which has had an impact on the cultural landscape including the music scene; and the growth of industries based on mass radio, television and recorded music.

All these these changes "(diluted) local traditions and (diverted) younger generations" from becoming involved in folk music because foreign, popular styles – including foreign music – came to be viewed as having more prestige, class and income.

Scratch bands and fungi music

Scratch bands, also known as *fungi bands* and formerly as *string bands*, are a distinctive form of folk ensemble. They have survived the decline of other Virgin Island folk traditions through adapting to newly imported instrumentation and songs, and becoming a part of a more general revival of interest in folk culture on the islands.

The name *scratch band* may be derived from the sound produced by scraping the *squash*, an instrument similar to the Puerto Rican *guiro* but larger, or from the word *squash* itself, used to refer to the bands first by American visitors and then by locals.

The traditional scratch band ensemble varied but always used a percussive instrument, either the *squash*, tambourine or a local form of double-headed barrel drum similar to the Dominican tambora, as well as an accordion, cane flute or violin as a melodic instrument.

String instruments were also common, including the banjo, ukulele or a six-string guitar. The *ass pipe*, made out of a car exhaust tube, often provided the bass and was played similar to the tuba.

Since about the 1980s, the instrumentation for scratch bands became more rigid. The alto saxophone became the most common melodic instrument, replaced sometimes by a silver flute, Conga drums, *squash*, electric guitar or bass guitar, and a *steel* (a triangle). Banjo or ukulele, keyboard and additional saxophones or other melodic instruments are more rarely found in modern bands.

The music of scratch bands are a type of folk music that dates back to the days of slavery.

The slaves on the islands used found objects to fashion into instruments; for example, by making strings out of twine salvaged from old sacks.

Lyrics traditionally functioned as oral history, spreading news and gossip.

Modern scratch bands play a wide range of dances including calypsos, boleros, quadrilles, international pop songs, merengues, mazurkas, waltzes, jigs and other styles.

They perform at church services, private parties, public festivals, local dances and fairs, christenings and weddings; they also perform for tourists.

The scratch band tradition remains most vibrant on St. Croix where bands such Bully & the Kafooners, Stanley & the Ten Sleepless Kninghts, and Blinky & the Roadmasters are well known.

Scratch bands are less common on St. Thomas and in

the British Virgin Islands, although the popular Elmo & The Sparkplugs come from Tortola, the largest island in the British Virgin Islands.

Quelbe

Quelbe is a form of topical folk song and is the official music of the Virgin Islands.

Quelbe is commonly performed by scratch bands, Stanley & the Ten Sleepless Nights being the most popular throughout the Virgin Islands.

Their folk origin was in individuals who sang the songs in informal settings, celebrations and festivals. The songs typically contained sexual innuendos and double entendres as well as other hidden meanings. Common topics included political events such as a boycott. One example from the early 20th century chastises a carousel owner for opposing a wage increase:

I rather walk and drink rum whole night
Before me go ride on LaBega Carousel
I rather walk, man, and drink rum whole night
Before me go ride on LaBega Carousel
You no hear what LaBega say
"The people no worth more than fifteen cent a day"
You no hear what LaBega say, man
"The people no worth more than half cent a day"

Other folk styles

The Virgin Islands tea meetings, the David and Goliath play and masquerade jig all probably came from elsewhere in the Caribbean.

The masquerade jig uses elements of theatre, dance, music and oratory, and functions as simple form of entertainment with improvised jigs alternated with humorous monologues.

Tea meetings are now only performed as

reconstructions in folkloric ensembles. Originally, they were evenings of speech-making, feasting and the singing of hymns and parlour songs.

The David and Goliath play features music, dance, theatre and dramatic and witty speeches based on the biblical plot of David and Goliath.

The Afro-Virgin Island *bamboula* tradition is now only performed in a reconstructed fashion. It was a style of song, drumming and folk dance performed by two drummers on one drum; one drummer used his hands and heel, and the other two sticks.

African-style dance and group songs with refrains were a constant part of this tradition, with verses frequently improvised by a soloist.

Even the name *bamboula* itself is of African origin. It may be of Mandinka – Mandingo – origin because of the similarity between the term *bamboula* and Bambara. In Mali and other parts of West Africa, the Mandinka – or Mandingo – are also known as Bambara.

Traditional Virgin Island folk music festivals were performed until the late 1950s. Masquerading (*mas'ing*) was an important tradition and consisted of groups wearing costumes based on a theme and playing melodies and rhythms that suggest their identity.

Instruments included a fife-and-drum ensemble that featured a cane fife; a double-headed bass drum known as *keg* or *boom-boom*; and a snare drum known as *kettledrum*.

The Virgin Island *cariso* tradition is extinct in a true folk context but remains an important symbol of Crucian culture and is performed by folkloric ensembles for educational and holiday events.

Carisos were still performed as late as the 1990s by several elderly singers, most famously Ethe McIntosh and Leona Watson.

Although similar to *quelbe* in some ways, *cariso* is more African in its melodic style, frequent sustained syllables and traditional performance context, namely women singing in groups in a call-response format. *Carisos*, like *quelbe*, commemorate historical events and spread news and opinions about important issues.

One particularly famous *cariso* dates to 1848 and documents the emancipation of the slaves; the first segment is the refrain, sung by a chorus, which is followed by a verse performed by a soloist singer:

Clear the road, all you clear the road,
Clear the road, let the slave them pass,
We a go for a-we freedom.

Hardship in the morning, suffering at night.
No one ever help us, it is only Father Ryan.
They bring we ya from Africa, that we bornin' land;
Bring we ya in slavery, in the land of Santa Cruz

Modern and recently imported styles

Until the mid-20th century, the Virgin Islands were to a large extent culturally isolated from international popular music.

In the 1960s, a growth in tourism caused an influx of immigrants to fill the service positions the tourism industry created. These immigrants brought with them many styles of popular music which were popularised by the growth of mass media in the islands including television and radio.

By the 1980s, the Virgin Islands was home to many imported styles, especially reggae, soca, merengue and rock.

Jazz, Western classical music and music theatre, along with international pop stars, were common mainstream interests, while the islands' youth formed bands and dance troupes that played styles popular across the Caribbean, such as reggae, steelpan and soca.

The large Puerto Rican population in the Virgin

Islands, as well as immigrants from the Dominican Republic, also made popular music from their homelands an integral part of the islands' music industry.

Calypso

The first calypso star from the Virgin Islands was Lloyd "Prince" Thomas who moved to New York City in the mid-1940s. He continued to perform for about 20 years.

Also, Charles Harris, the Mighty Zebra who was a well-known Trinidadian calypsonian, performed in the Virgin Islands in the 1950s with great success. He went to the Virgin Islands for the Carnival in 1952 and stayed, playing at the Virgin Isles Hotel with the LaMotta Brothers Band.

The LaMotta Band, led by Bill LaMotta, was a very popular group that recorded several albums and backed Mighty Zebra on a 1957 album for RCA Records.

The remaining major early calypso band from the Virgin Islands was the Fabulous McClevertys who toured widely across the East Coast of the United States at the height of the calypso craze in the late 1950s.

Another popular Virgin Islands calypsonian is Irvin "Brownie" Brown who has hosted the islands' Carnival and has been a leading singer, radio entertainer, MC and drummer for many years. Originally from St. Thomas, he learned the timbales as a young man and joined his uncle's hotel band in 1949 or 1950.

The band soon began performing in Florida and elsewhere, and Brownie became known as a calypso singer while also learning bongos, congas and a trap set. They recorded for Monogram and then for Art Records with Mighty Panther and the Haitian singer Calypso Mama.

Brownie's return to St. Thomas was followed by joining up with Milo & the Kings, a well-known band, for whom he was a percussion for seventeen years, recording a number of albums and touring across North America and the Caribbean.

He began working as a DJ for the WSTA radio station in 1966 and continued to do so for more than 30 years. He also had a regular talk show with calypso performances. The show was called *The Original Side of Walter and Brownie*.

Soca

The Virgin Islands has been home to a number of well-known soca bands. Among the oldest and most respected are Milo & the Kings, Seventeen Plus (17+). Seventeen Plus can be used as the standard for all modern soca bands since 1970.

Others were the Jam Band, formerly Eddie & the Movements, and the Imagination Brass. The Jam Band were the Road March Champions 20 times.

More recent popular bands include VIO International; World Famous Xpress Band which was the St. Croix Festival's 2006-2007 Road March Champions; Starlites; and the Musically Dangerous Xtaushun Band who were the St. Croix Festival two-time Road March Champions. Recently, the JDPP Jammerz have rapidly made a name for themselves and even won the 2007 St. Thomas Carnival Road March with their song "Bunny Train."

Another largely popular soca band since the 2000s on St Thomas is the "P'your Passion Band." The original "Jam Band" has also slowed up with the death of the band's main front man "Nick 'Daddy' Friday" who died in 2005.

Popular Virgin Islands bands to date include De Fabulous Stroka Band, Hyvoltage Band, Code 9, Xpress Band, Jam Band, Jam Tyme, UMB Soldiers, JDPP Jammerz, Rupsion Band, Stylee Band, and the Xtaushun Band.

The most popular Virgin Islands band and a band before its time, is Seventeen Plus (17+). With the inception of the "riddim box," the electronic drum machine, 17+ was one of the first bands in the region to master its use as expressed in Seventeen Plus's New Style. It demonstrated the full use of the electronic keyboard, drum machines, vocals and a bass line working together to set the standard for all bands of the electronic drum machine era.

Reggae

Reggae has been flourishing in the Virgin Islands, especially on the island of St. Croix, for a long time.

The Virgin Islands' reggae has achieved much popularity throughout the Lesser Antilles, Puerto Rico, the United States, South America and Europe.

Prominent reggae artists from the Virgin Islands include Pressure, Midnite, Dezarie, Army, Abja, De Apostle, Niyorah, Emanuel, Bambu Station, Inner Visions, Sabbattical Ahdah, Eno, Revalation, Iba Wicked, Jah Rubal and many others.

The reggae music of St. Croix has a distinct "roots" feeling and is strongly rooted in Rastafari.

A prominent reggae label in St. Croix is I Grade Records which has released countless Midnite recordings, two Dezarie albums, two Niyorah albums, Army albums and Abja albums.

Bambu Station guitarist Tuff Lion, along with Laurent Alfred and Kenyatta Itola of I Grade Records, produce many of the tracks.

St. Croix also has a popular reggae radio station, WSTX 100.3 FM which features Virgin Islands' reggae.

Dance

In contemporary Virgin Islands society, there are various dance traditions, given its history of migration.

The dances most commonly associated with indigenous Virgin Island culture are *quadrille* which is also performed in many other Caribbean islands; and *bamboula*.

Other dances include bachata, meringue and salsa which were brought to the islands by immigrants from Puerto Rico and the Dominican Republic. They all have African elements.

Religion

Christianity is the leading religion in the Virgin Islands. There are Catholics and Protestants of various denominations.

As in many other Caribbean islands, there is a significant Rastafari presence.

There are also small communities of Muslims, Hindus, Buddhists and other eastern religions.

Language

The official language of both the U.S. and British Virgin Islands is English. However, Virgin Islands Creole is the main spoken dialect in informal, daily usage. And because of immigration from other Caribbean islands, use of Spanish and to a lesser degree French and French Creole has increased during the last few decades.

Danish was never use a language on the main islands in the Virgin Islands because most of the plantation and slave owners were not Danish. They were Dutch of English.

In terms of articulation, English is often barked by locals, with a quick creole accent; a linguistic feature some non-belongers visiting the islands, including some who live there, may consider to be an anomaly.

Virgin Islands Creole

Virgin Islands Creole, known in the Netherlands Antilles as Netherlands Antilles Creole, is an English-based creole spoken in the Virgin Islands and windward Netherlands Antilles in the Caribbean.
Virgin Islands Creole is not to be confused with Negerhollands, a Dutch-based creole that was once spoken in the Danish West Indies which is now the U.S. Virgin Islands after the United States bought the islands from the Danish government.

History

Virgin Islands Creole evolved when enslaved Africans, unable to communicate with each other and their masters because they were taken from different parts of Africa – especially West Africa – where they spoke different languages, created a new English-based dialect with West African-derived words and grammatical structure.

St. Thomas and St. John had a European population of mainly Dutch origin. African slaves who lived there created a Dutch-based creole, known as Negerhollands which is now an extinct language.

Negerhollands was in mainstream usage on St. Thomas and St. John until the 19th century when the British occupied the Danish West Indies from 1801 to 1802 and 1807 to 1815.

As English became preferred as a trade and business language in the busy port of Charlotte Amalie, Virgin Islands Creole became established in preference to Negerhollands. But a segment of the population continued to use Negerhollands well into the 20th century.

Unlike the European population of the other Danish West Indian islands, that of St. Croix was mostly of

English, Irish and Scottish origin, which led to African slaves' developing an English-based creole throughout the 18th and 19th centuries. By the 19th century, Virgin Islands Creole was spoken on St. Thomas and St. John as Negerhollands was fading away. By the end of the 19th century, the English creole completely replaced Negerhollands as the native dialect of what is now the United States Virgin Islands.

Parallel development was taking place in what is today the British Virgin Islands. Virgin Islands Creole was evolving based on the English language and West African languages.

The British took over the islands from the Dutch in 1672. Enslaved Africans were taken to work on plantations on Tortola and Virgin Gorda islands where they, like those on St. Croix 40 miles away, also developed an English-based creole.

In one form or the other, Virgin Islands Creole exists today as the native dialect of the U.S. and British Virgin Islands and is spoken with slight variations from island-to-island. And although the two territories are politically separate, British and American, they share a common Virgin Islands culture, similar history based on colonialism and slavery, and some common bloodlines.

The English-based creoles spoken on the islands of Saint Martin, Sint Eustatius, and Saba, are considered by linguists to be a form of Virgin Islands Creole, albeit spoken with a slightly different accent.

Language use and perceptions

Virgin Islands Creole does not have the status of an official language. It's strictly informal and is a constantly changing dialect filled with various slang terms and idioms.

The language of government, education and the media

is American English in the U.S. Virgin Islands and British English in the British Virgin Islands.

In the Virgin Islands, a post-creole speech continuum exists in which there are two extremes – standard English known as the *acrolect* and the creole in its most raw form known as the *basilect*.

And due to constant contact between standard English and Virgin Islands Creole in local society, there are also many speech varieties – between the two extremes – known as *mesolects*.

Most native Virgin Islanders can easily manoeuvre this continuum depending on their mood, subject matter, or their addressee.

Virgin Islands Creole has different forms that vary by the age of the speaker. Many words and expressions are known only by older Virgin Islanders. There are also relatively newer words and expressions known only to younger Virgin Islanders.

The dialect continues to undergo changes in a "post-creole" environment. Its most modern form is mainly derived from traditional Virgin Islands Creole terms, idioms, proverbs and sentence structure, with influences from African-American and Jamaican idioms due to the prevalence of African-American and Jamaican mainstream pop culture in the Virgin Islands.

The variant of Virgin Islands Creole spoken on St. Croix, known as *Crucian*, contains many Spanish-derived words due to St. Croix's large ethnic Puerto Rican population.

As in other Caribbean creoles, proverbs are prevalent in Virgin Islands Creole. However, in 2004, a linguistic study group in cooperation with the University of Puerto Rico's Rio Piedras campus found that many old proverbs in the Crucian dialect, common among older generations, have faded away and are not generally known among many young Crucians.

Many Virgin Islanders who migrate to the United

States often return with American-influenced speech patterns – colloquially known as *yankin'* – that influence local speech of their peer groups.

These changes, as well as the perception held by many older Virgin Islanders that the dialect is currently undergoing decreolisation, have inspired debates on whether the dialect spoken by young Virgin Islanders today is in fact the true Virgin Islands Creole.

Like most Caribbean dialects, the use of Virgin Islands Creole can vary depending on socioeconomic class. The middle and upper classes tend to speak it informally among friends and at home, but code switch to Standard English in the professional sphere. The lower socioeconomic classes tend to use the dialect in almost every aspect of daily life.

In the U.S. Virgin Islands, there has been an underlying negative pressure on Virgin Islanders to eliminate their dialect due to Americanisation since the United States acquired the islands from Denmark in 1917.

Standard American English is associated with social mobility as it's widely used in business and professional circles in the U.S. Virgin Islands. Virgin Islands Creole, although appreciated for its cultural value and widely used informally, is often seen as an impediment to economic and educational progress.

The majority of Virgin Islanders speak Virgin Islands Creole. However, due to immigration from the rest of the Caribbean and the United States, some Virgin Islands residents do not speak the dialect. Most non-native longtime residents can understand spoken Virgin Islands Creole, even if not fluent in speaking themselves.

In the Virgin Islands, the dialect is rarely referred to as a creole since, locally, "creole" – as well as "patois" – usually refers to the French-based creoles spoken by St. Lucian, Dominican – from Dominica, *not* from the Dominican Republic – and Haitian immigrants.

Instead, Virgin Islanders tend to refer to the dialect by

their native island – for example, "Crucian dialect" spoken on St. Croix; "Thomian dialect" spoken on St. Thomas, and "Tortolian dialect" spoken on Tortola.

As with other Caribbean creoles, Virgin Islands Creole is generally unwritten. However, local authors often write in the creole, and young Virgin Islanders tend to write in this language when communicating over the Internet. Because no standard spelling system exists in Virgin Islands Creole, those who attempt to write it use English orthography.

The prevailing sentiment is that Virgin Islands Creole can not be learned like a standard language but is acquired only through having spent one's formative years in the Virgin Islands. Attempts by Virgin Islands non-native residents to speak the dialect, even out of respect, are often met with disapproval.

Grammatical structure and pronunciation

As with other Caribbean creoles, Virgin Islands Creole has a smaller set of pronouns than English. And conjugations occur less often. For example, the English phrase "I gave it to her" would translate to "I gi' 'e to she" in Virgin Islands Creole.

Another common pattern found in Virgin Islands Creole is the absence of the letter "s" in the plural, possessive and third person present tense.

Differences from English

The pronunciation differs from Standard English in various ways. Virgin Islands accents are somewhat similar to those of other Caribbean countries, especially those in the Leeward Islands and Belize but are also unique in many ways.

As in most Anglophone Caribbean dialects, in Virgin

Islands Creole, dental fricatives (the "-th" sound) are often omitted from speech, and replaced by dental stops (the "-t" sound).

The vowel pronunciation of Virgin Islands Creole can widely differ from Standard English. For example, the suffix "er" in English, /ər/ in Standard English, is pronounced /æ/ (for example: *computer* is pronounced [komputæ] ("computah"); and *never* is pronounced [nevæ] ("nevah"). Not all words ending in "er" are pronounced in this way.

Variations in grammar and speech among islands

Local speech varies among each of the U.S. and British Virgin Islands. It is commonplace for such differences to be pointed out in jest when Virgin Islanders of different islands congregate. For example, the pronunciation of the standard English phrase "come here" would be *come ya* on St. Croix, and *come heh* on St. Thomas, St. John and the British Virgin Islands.

In addition, the Virgin Islands Creole form of the word "car" is *cyar* on St. Croix and *cah* on St. Thomas, St. John and the British Virgin Islands. These two anomalies are due to Irish influence on St. Croix during the Danish colonial period.

Vowel sounds can also widely differ between islands. For example, the word "special" is usually pronounced *speshahl* on St. Croix and *speshuhl* on St. Thomas, St. John and the British Virgin Islands. "Island" is usually pronounced *islahn'* on St. Croix and *isluhn'* on St. Thomas, St. John and the British Virgin Islands.

Another notable difference is the usage of the term *deh*, the Virgin Islands Creole form of the standard English adverb "there."

On St. Croix, an additional *deh* is often added, forming

the phrase *deh-deh*. Such usage is found in many Caribbean islands outside the Virgin Islands, as well. There are many instances where words and phrases – especially slang – that exist on one island may not exist on another.

In addition, the Virgin Islands Creole spoken on St. Croix is often described as being more "raw" – or more distant from standard English – than those of the other Virgin Islands.

Examples of Virgin Islands Creole Proverbs

"Who don't hear does feel."

"What yoh do in de dark does come to light."

"Time longer dan twine."

"Every skin teeth ain' a grin."

"Monkey know wha' tree to clime."

"Do for do ain' no obeah."

Chapter Six:

Cayman Islands

The Cayman Islands is a British Overseas Territory located in the western Caribbean Sea.

The territory comprises the islands of Grand Cayman, Cayman Brac, and Little Cayman located south of Cuba and northwest of Jamaica. It's considered a part of the geographic Western Caribbean Zone.

The territory is a major offshore financial centre in the Caribbean.

History

The Cayman Islands were sighted by Christopher Columbus on 10 May 1503 on his fourth and final voyage to the New World. He named the islands *Las Tortugas* after the numerous sea turtles there.

The first recorded English visitor to the islands was Sir

Francis Drake who landed there in 1586 and named them the Cayman Islands after "caiman," the Neo-Taino nations' term for alligator.

The first recorded permanent inhabitant of the Cayman Islands, Isaac Bodden, was born on Grand Cayman around 1661. He was the grandson of the original settler named Bodden who was probably one of Oliver Cromwell's soldiers at the taking of Jamaica in 1655.

The Cayman Islands remained largely uninhabited until the 17th century.

A variety of people settled on the islands, including pirates, refugees from the Spanish Inquisition, shipwrecked sailors, deserters from Oliver Cromwell's army in Jamaica, and slaves.

The majority of Caymanians are of African and British descent, with considerable interracial mixing.

Great Britain took formal control of the Cayman Islands, along with Jamaica, under the Treaty of Madrid in 1670.

Following several unsuccessful attempts, permanent settlement of the islands began in the 1730s. The islands, along with nearby Jamaica, were captured from the Spanish Empire, then ceded to England under the Treaty of Madrid (1670). They were governed as a single colony with Jamaica until 1962 when they became a separate British Overseas Territory and Jamaica became an independent Commonwealth realm.

The island of Grand Cayman, which lies largely unprotected at sea level, was hit by Hurricane Ivan on 11 and 12 September 2004. The hurricane destroyed many buildings and damaged 90 per cent of them. Power, water and communications were all disrupted in some areas for months. Ivan was the worst hurricane to hit the islands in 86 years.

However, Grand Cayman began a major rebuilding process and within two years its infrastructure was nearly returned to pre-hurricane levels.

The Cayman Islands have the dubious honour, and distinction, of having experienced the most hurricane strikes in history.

Due to the proximity of the islands, more hurricane and tropical systems have affected the Cayman Islands than any other region in the Atlantic basin, being brushed or directly hit, on average, every 2.23 years.

The Cayman Islands have been a tax-exempt destination for many years. Legend has it that in 1788 Caymanians rescued the crews of a Jamaican merchant ship convoy which had struck a reef at Gun Bay during a hurricane, and that the Caymanians were rewarded with King George III's promise to never again impose a tax.

Geography

The Cayman Islands is a three-island archipelago. Located 150 miles south of Cuba and 167 miles northwest of Jamaica, and between Cuba and Central America, the islands have a land area of 101.2 square miles.

They have almost the same area as the islands of Saint Kitts and Nevis which are also located in the Caribbean. The Cayman Islands are only 1.2 square miles larger than Saint Kitts and Nevis. And they have a coastline of 99 miles.

The highest point in the Cayman Islands is The Bluff, a limestone outcrop 155 feet high on the eastern end of eastern Cayman Brac which itself was named for The Bluff. "Brac" is Gaelic for "bluff."

The Cayman Islands are located in the western Caribbean Sea and are the peaks of a massive underwater ridge known as the Cayman Trench – or Trough – standing 8,000 feet from the sea floor which barely exceeds the surface.

Grand Cayman is by far the biggest island with an area of 76 square miles. The two "Sister Islands" of Cayman Brac and Little Cayman are located about 80 miles east of

Grand Cayman and have areas of 14 square miles and 10 square miles, respectively.

All three islands are mostly flat. One notable exception to this is The Bluff on Cayman Brac's eastern part.

Climate

The Cayman Islands have a tropical marine climate with a wet season of warm, rainy summers (May to October) and a dry season of relatively cool winters (November to April).

The terrain is mostly a low-lying limestone base surrounded by coral reefs.

A major natural hazard is the tropical cyclones which form during the Atlantic hurricane season from July to November.

Environmental issues

A major environmental issue is the lack of fresh water resources. Drinking water supplies must be met by rainwater catchment and desalination.

Demographics

The Cayman Islands have more registered businesses than they have people.

The latest population estimate of the Cayman Islands is about 60,000, representing a mix of more than 100 nationalities. Out of that number, about half are of Caymanian descent.

About 60 per cent of the population is of mixed race – mostly mixed African-European. Of the remaining 40 per cent, about half are of European descent and half are of African descent.

The islands are almost exclusively Christian, with large numbers of Presbyterians and Catholics.

Caymanians enjoy the highest standard of living in the Caribbean.

The vast majority of the population resides on Grand Cayman, followed by Cayman Brac and Little Cayman, respectively.

The capital of the Cayman Islands is George Town. It's located on the southwest coast of Grand Cayman.

According to the Islands' Economics and Statistics Office (ESO), the resident population of the Cayman Islands is 60,456 persons.

The population is concentrated in the three (south-)western districts: George Town, the capital; West Bay, and Bodden Town.

The three districts have a population density many times higher than all the remaining districts.

Economy

With an average income of around KYD$42,000, Caymanians enjoy the highest standard of living in the Caribbean.

According to the *CIA World Facybook*, the Cayman Islands GDP per capita is the 12th highest in the world.

The islands print their own currency, the Cayman Islands Dollar (KYD) which is pegged to the U.S. dollar at a fixed rate of 1 KYD = 1.25 USD.

The government's primary source of income is indirect taxation: there is no income tax, capital gains tax, or corporation tax.

An import duty of 5% to 20% is levied against goods imported into the islands. Few goods are exempt; notable examples include books, cameras and infant formula.

The economy of the Cayman Islands is mainly fuelled by the tourism sector and by the financial sector which together represent 70 - 80 per cent of the country's gross domestic product (GDP).

The Cayman Island Investment Bureau, a government agency, has been established with the mandate of promoting investment and economic development in the territory.

The emergence of what are now considered the Cayman Islands' "twin pillars of economic development" – tourism and international finance – started in the 1950s with the introduction of modern transport and telecommunications.

History of the islands' economy

From the earliest settlement of the Cayman Islands, economic activity was hindered by isolation and a limited natural resource base. The harvesting of sea turtles to resupply passing sailing ships was the first major economic activity on the islands but local stocks were depleted by the 1790s.

Agriculture, while sufficient to support the small early settler population, has always been limited by the scarcity of available land.

Fishing shipbuilding, and cotton production boosted the economy during the early days of settlement. In addition, settlers scavenged shipwreck remains from the surrounding coral reefs.

The boom in the Cayman Islands' international finance industry can also be at least partly attributed to the British overseas territory having no direct taxation.

A popular legend attributes the tax-free status to the heroic acts of the inhabitants during a maritime tragedy in 1794, often referred to as "Wreck of the Ten Sails."

The wreck involved nine British merchant vessels and their naval escort, the frigate HMS Convert, that ran aground on the reefs off Grand Cayman. Due to the rescue efforts by the Caymanians using canoes, the loss of life was limited to eight.

However, records from the colonial era indicate that Cayman Islands, then a dependency of Jamaica, was not tax-exempt during the period that followed.

In 1803, the inhabitants signed a petition addressed to the Jamaican governor asking him to grant them a tax exemption from the "Transient Tax on Wreck Goods."

International finance and tourism

The Cayman Islands' tax-free status has attracted numerous banks and other companies to its shores.

More than 40,000 companies were registered in the Cayman Islands as of 2000, including almost 600 banks and trust companies with banking assets exceeding $500 billion.

It's a tax haven that continues to attract businesses from all parts of the world. Large corporations based in the Cayman Islands include Seagate Technology, Semiconductor Manufacturing International Corporation (SMIC), Garmin Ltd. and Transocean Inc.

The Cayman Islands Stock Exchange was opened in 1997.

Tourism is also a mainstay of the economy, accounting for about 70% of GDP and 75% of foreign currency earnings.

The tourist industry is aimed at the luxury market and caters mainly to visitors from North America. Unspoiled beaches, duty-free shopping, scuba diving, and deep-sea fishing draw almost a million visitors to the islands each year. Due to the well-developed tourist industry, many citizens work in service jobs in that sector.

One of Grand Cayman's (GCM's) main attractions is Seven Mile Beach on which a number of the island's hotels and resorts are located. Historical sites in GCM such as Pedro St. James Castle in Bodden Town also attract visitors. Tourists also visit the Sister Islands, Little Cayman and Cayman Brac.

All three islands offer scuba diving, and the Caymans are home to several snorkeling locations where tourists can swim with stingrays. One of these famous locations is Stingray City, Grand Cayman.

There are two shipwrecks off the shores of Cayman Brac including the MV Keith Tibbetts.

Other Grand Cayman tourist attractions include the Ironshore landscape of Hell, the 23-acre marine theme park Boatswain's Beach, also home of the Cayman Turtle Farm, the production of gourmet sea salt, and the Mastic Trail, a hiking trail through the forests in the centre of the island.

The National Trust for the Cayman Islands provides guided tours weekly on the Mastic Trail and other locations.

The Cayman Islands are a major international financial centre. The biggest sectors are "banking, hedge fund formation and investment, structured finance and securitization, captive insurance, and general corporate activities."

Regulation and supervision of the financial services industry is the responsibility of the Cayman Islands Monetary Authority (CIMA).

The Cayman Islands are the fifth-largest banking centre in the world with $1.5 trillion in banking liabilities. There are 279 banks (as of June 2008), 19 of which are licensed to conduct banking activities with domestic (Cayman-based) and international clients. The remaining 260 are licensed to operate on an international basis with only limited domestic activity.

One reason for the Cayman Islands' success as an offshore financial centre has been the concentration of top-quality service providers. These include leading global financial institutions such as UBS and Goldman Sachs, over 80 administrators, leading accountancy practices including the Big Four auditors, and offshore law practices including Maples & Calder and Ogier.

Since the introduction of the Mutual Funds Law in 1993 which has been copied by jurisdictions around the world, the Cayman Islands have grown to be the world's leading offshore hedge fund jurisdiction. In June 2008 it passed 10,000 hedge fund registrations. And over the year ending June 2008, the Cayman Islands Monetary Authority (CIMA) reported a net growth rate of 12% for hedge funds.

Starting in the mid-late 1990s, offshore financial centres such as the Cayman Islands came under increasing pressure from the OECD for their allegedly harmful tax regimes. The OECD wished to prevent low-tax regimes from having an advantage in the global marketplace.

The OECD threatened to place the Cayman Islands and other financial centres on a "black list" and impose sanctions against them.

However, the Cayman Islands successfully avoided being placed on the OECD black list in 2000 by committing to regulatory reform to improve transparency and begin information exchange with OECD member countries about their citizens.

In 2004, under pressure from the United Kingdom, the Cayman Islands agreed in principle to implement the European Union Savings Directive (EUSD) but only after securing some important benefits for the financial services industry in the Cayman Islands.

As the Cayman Islands are not subject to European Union (EU) laws, implementation of the EUSD is by way of bilateral agreements between each EU member state and the Cayman Islands.

The government of the Cayman Islands agreed on a model agreement which set out how the EUSD would be implemented with the Cayman Islands.

A report published by the International monetary Fund (IMF) in March 2005 assessing supervision and regulation in the Cayman Islands' banking, insurance and securities industries, as well as its money laundering regime, recognised the jurisdiction's comprehensive regulatory and compliance frameworks. "An extensive program of legislative, rule and guideline development has introduced an increasingly effective system of regulation, both formalizing earlier practices and introducing enhanced procedures," noted IMF assessors.

The report further stated that "the supervisory system benefits from a well-developed banking infrastructure with an internationally experienced and qualified workforce as well as experienced lawyers, accountants and auditors," adding that "the overall compliance culture within Cayman is very strong, including the compliance culture related to AML (anti-money laundering) obligations."

On May 4, 2009, United States President Barack Obama declared his intentions to curb the use of financial centres by multinational corporations. In his speech, he singled out the Cayman Islands as a tax shelter. The next day, the Cayman Island Financial Services Association submitted an open letter to President Obama detailing The Caymans' role in international finance and its value to the US financial system.

Natural resources

Natural resources include fish and a climate and beaches that foster tourism which is the islands' major industry. A 2005 estimate of land use determined that the Cayman Islands had 3.85 per cent arable land and no permanent crops.

Standard of living

Because the islands cannot produce enough goods to support the population, about 90% of their food and consumer goods must be imported.

In addition, the islands have few natural fresh water resources. Desalination of sea water is used to solve the problem of water shortage.

Despite those challenges, the Caymanians enjoy one of the highest outputs per capita and one of the highest standards of living in the world. The Cayman Islands produces gourmet sea salt.

Education is compulsory to the age of 16 and is free to all Caymanian children. Most schools follow the British educational system.

Ten primary schools, one special education school, a high school and a middle school (junior high school) are operated by the government together with three private high schools. In addition, there is a law school, a university-college and a medical school.

Labour

The Cayman Islands has a small population and therefore a limited work force. Work permits may therefore be granted to foreigners. On average, there have been more than 21,000 foreigners holding valid work permits.

Work permits for non-citizens

In order to work in the Cayman Islands as a non-citizen, a work permit is required. This involves passing a police background check and a health check.

A prospective immigrant worker will not be granted a permit if he or she tests positive for syphilis or HIV or has other medical conditions which make him/her ineligible for entry into the islands to work or live.

A permit may be granted to individuals on special work.

A foreigner must first have a job in order to move to the Cayman Islands. The employer applies and pays for the work permit. Work permits are not granted to foreigners who are in the Cayman Islands unless it is a renewal. The Cayman Islands Immigration Department requires foreigners to remain out of the country until their work permit has been approved.

The Cayman Islands presently imposes a controversial "rollover" policy in relation to expatriate workers who require a work permit.

Non-Caymanians are only permitted to reside and work within the territory for a maximum of seven years – non-renewable – unless they satisfy the criteria of key employees. The policy has been the subject of some controversy within the press. Law firms have been particularly upset by the recruitment difficulties that it has caused. Other less well-remunerated employment sectors have been affected as well.

Concerns about safety have been expressed by diving instructors and realtors have also expressed concerns. Others support the rollover as necessary to protect Caymanian identity in the face of large immigration of expatriate workers.

Concerns have been expressed that in the long term, the policy may damage the preeminence of the Cayman Islands as an offshore financial centre by making it difficult to recruit and retain experienced staff from onshore financial centres.

Government employees are no longer exempt from this "rollover" policy according to this report in a local newspaper. The governor has decided to use his constitutional powers, which give him absolute control for the disposition of civil service employees, to determine which expatriate civil servants are dismissed after seven years service and which are not.

This policy is enshrined in the Immigration Law (2003 revision), written by the UDP government, and subsequently enforced by the PPM government. Both governments agree to the term limits on foreign workers, and the majority of Caymanians also agree it is necessary to protect local culture and heritage from being eroded by a large number of foreigners gaining residency and citizenship.

Taxation

There is no direct taxation imposed on residents and Cayman Islands companies. The government receives the majority of its income from indirect taxation.

Duty is levied against most imported goods, which is typically in the range of 22% to 25%. Some items are exempted like baby formula, books, cameras and certain items at a reduced rate of 5%. Duty on automobiles depends on the age and value and can be up to 40% for expensive models.

Financial institutions that operate in the islands are charged a flat licensing fee by the government, in addition to work permit fees on foreign labour.

A 10% government tax is placed on all tourist accommodations in addition to a small fee each tourist pays upon entering on the Cayman Islands.

Foreign relations

Foreign policy is controlled by the United Kingdom as the islands are not an independent nation. They're an integral part of the UK officially classified as its overseas territory.

Although in its early days the Cayman Islands' most important relationships were with Britain and Jamaica, a relationship with the United States has developed in recent years because of the islands' economic dependence on its giant partner.

The Cayman Islands are not involved in any major international disputes. But they have come under criticism because of the use of their territory for narcotics trafficking and money laundering.

In an attempt to address the problem, the government entered into the Narcotics Agreement of 1984 and the Mutual Legal Assistance Treaty of 1986 with the United States in order to reduce the use of their facilities associated with these activities.

In more recent years, the Cayman Islands have stepped up the fight against money laundering by limiting banking secrecy, introducing requirements for customer identification and record keeping, and requiring banks to cooperate with foreign investigators.

Due to their status as an overseas territory of the UK, the Cayman Islands have no representation either in the United Nations or in most other international organizations.

However, as a territorial entity with legal status in the international system, the Cayman Islands participates in some international organisations as an associate member of Caricom and UNESCO, and as a member of a sub-bureau of Interpol.

The defence and internal security of the Cayman Islands is the responsibility of the United Kingdom.

Education

The Cayman Islands Education Department operates state schools. Caymanian children are entitled to free primary and secondary education. Various churches and private foundations operate several private schools that offer American- and British-based studies starting from nursery up to A Level (Advanced Level; a classification applicable to school systems in the UK and in its former colonies in Africa, Asia and elsewhere).

The University College of the Cayman Islands is located in George Town on Grand Cayman and is the only government-run university on the island.

Another school, the International College of the Cayman Islands is a private college and is located in Newlands, Grand Cayman, about seven miles east of George Town. The college was established in 1970 and offers Associate's, Bachelor's and postgraduate degree programmes.

Grand Cayman is also home to St. Matthew's University which includes a medical school and a school of veterinary medicine.

The Cayman Islands Law School, which is a branch of the University of Liverpool in the UK, is also based on Grand Cayman. Located in George Town, the law school has been in operation since 1982.

The Cayman Islands Civil Service College (CICSC), a unit of the Cayman Islands government organised under the Portfolio of the Civil Service, is also located in Grand Cayman. It's on the same premises with University College of the Cayman Islands in a building on the south side of the campus and intends to offer degree programmes and continuing education in various fields. The college is also intended to be a government research centre. It opened in autumn 2007.

Music

The Cayman Islands is home to a number of bands which range from concert bands to steel bands. Modern forms of music composed in Cayman include reggae, soca, hip-hop, and rhythm and blues (R&B).

Traditional Caymanian music was a "Kitchen band" which was composed of a fiddle, drum, spoon and bottle, washboard, and possibly a harmonica or guitar. There is currently a band of Caymanians who perform as the

Kitchen Band during cultural celebrations such as CayFest or Heritage Days during Pirate's Week. This type of music is often fast-paced and bears similarities to country and calypso music.

The music of the Cayman Islands includes a wide selection of international pop music as well as unique folk styles.

The Cayman National National Cultural Foundation established in 1984 helps to preserve and promote Cayman folk music including the organisation of festivals such as Cayman Islands International Storytelling Festival, the Cayman JazzFest, Seafarers Festival, and Cayfest.

There is also a Pirate's Week Festival.

The Cayman JazzFest, founded in 2004, is a well-known jazz festival which draws on the islands' "deep connection" with jazz.

The official national anthem of the Cayman Islands is "God Save the Queen." "Beloved Isle Cayman," words and music by organist Leila Ross-Shier, is the official national song.

The fiddle is a popular folk instrument.

Christmas music is an important part of the Cayman folk tradition. It consists of *serenading*, or group singing of Christmas carols on Christmas Eve. Instruments include the fiddle, accordion, mouth organ, *grater*, and drums.

Chapter Seven:

Dominica

Dominica is officially known as the Commonwealth of Dominica.

It's located in the Caribbean Sea north-northwest of Guadeloupe. To the southeast is Martinique.

It has an area of 291 square miles and a population of about 73,000. Roseau is its capital.

The highest point in the country is Morne Diablotins which is 4,747 feet high.

The island nation is nicknamed the "Nature Isle of the Caribbean" for its seemingly unspoiled natural beauty.

It's the youngest island in the Lesser Antilles and is still being formed by geothermal-volcanic activity, as evidenced by the world's second-largest boiling lake.

The island has lush mountainous rain forests. And it gets heavy rainfall inland.

Dominica's economy is heavily dependent on tourism

and agriculture.

Christopher Columbus named the island after the day of the week on which he spotted it, a Sunday (*dominica* in Latin), November 3, 1493.

In the next hundred years after Columbus' landing, Dominica remained isolated with its Carib population. More Caribs settled there after being driven from surrounding islands by Europeans who entered the region.

France formally ceded possession of Dominica to the United Kingdom in 1763. The United Kingdom then set up a government and made the island a colony in 1805.

The emancipation of African slaves occurred throughout the British empire in 1834 and, in 1838, Dominica became the first British Caribbean colony to have a legislature controlled by an African majority.

In 1896, the United Kingdom resumed governmental control of Dominica, turning it into a crown colony.

Half a century later, from 1958 to 1962, Dominica became a province of the short-lived West Indies Federation.

In 1978, Dominica became an independent nation.

The official language is English because it was a British colony. But a French creole is spoken by many, especially people of older generations.

The demonym or adjective is "Dominican" in English, same as that for the Dominican Republic which is a different country and former Spanish colony. But unlike the "Dom*i*nican" Republic in which the stress is on the first "i," the stress is on the second "i" in the case of "Domin*i*ca."

History

In 1635, France claimed Dominica. Shortly thereafter, French missionaries became the first Europeans to settle on the island. But Carib resistance continued and, in 1660, the French and the British agreed that both Dominica and

St. Vincent should be abandoned.

Dominica was officially neutral during the next century. But attraction of its resources remained. Rival expeditions of British and French foresters started harvesting timber in the early part of the 18th century.

Largely because of Dominica's position between Martinique and Guadeloupe, France eventually became predominant, and a French settlement was established on the island.

As part of the 1763 Treaty of Paris that ended the Seven Years' War, the island became a British possession.

In 1778, during the American Revolutionary War, the French mounted a successful invasion of Dominica with the active cooperation of the local French settlers on the island.

The 1783 Treaty of Paris which ended the war returned the island to Britain. French invasions in 1795 and 1805 ended in failure.

In 1763, the British established a legislative assembly representing only the white population.

In 1831, reflecting a liberalisation of official British racial attitudes, the Brown Privilege Bill conferred political and social rights on free non-whites. Three Africans – descendants of African slaves on the island – were elected to the legislative assembly the following year.

In 1838 following the abolition of slavery, Dominica became the only British Caribbean colony to have an African-controlled legislature in the 19th century.

Most African legislators were smallholders or merchants who held economic and social views diametrically opposed to the interests of the small, wealthy English planter class. Reacting to a perceived threat, the planters lobbied for more direct British rule.

In 1865, after much agitation and tension, the colonial office replaced the elective assembly with one that had one-half of members who were elected and one-half who were appointed.

British planters on the island allied themselves with the colonial administrators to outmanoeuvre the elected legislators on numerous occasions.

In 1871, Dominica became part of the Leeward Island Federation. And the power of the African population progressively eroded.

Crown colony government was re-established in 1896. All political rights for the vast majority of the population – who were African – were effectively curtailed. Development aid, offered as compensation for disenfranchisement, proved to have a negligible effect.

Following World War I, an upsurge of political consciousness throughout the Caribbean led to the formation of the Representative Government Association. Marshalling public frustration with the lack of a voice in the governing of Dominica, this group won one-third of the popularly elected seats of the legislative assembly in 1924 and one-half in 1936.

Shortly thereafter, Dominica was transferred from the Leeward Island Administration and was governed as part of the Windwards until 1958 when it joined the short-lived West Indies Federation.

After the federation dissolved, Dominica became an associated state of the United Kingdom in 1967 and formally took responsibility for its internal affairs.

On November 3, 1978, the Commonwealth of Dominica won independence from the United Kingdom.

But independence did little to solve problems stemming from centuries of economic underdevelopment and, in mid-1979, political discontent led to the formation of an interim government. It was replaced after the 1980 elections by a government led by the Dominica Freedom Party under Prime Minister Eugenia Charles who became the Caribbean's first female prime minister.

Chronic economic problems were compounded by the severe impact of hurricanes in 1979 and in 1980.

In 1981 Dominica was threatened with a takeover by

mercenaries. A group of right-wing mercenaries led by Mike Perdue of Houston and Wolfgang Droege of Toronto attempted to overthrow the government of Eugenia Charles.

The North American mercenary group wanted to help ex-Prime Minister Patrick John and his Dominica Defence Force regain control of the island in exchange for control over the island's future development, turning the island into a virtual colony or a personal estate of the mercenaries and their cohorts. The offensive was codenamed Operation Red Dog.

But the plan failed. And the ship hired to transport the invaders never even left for the mission, following a tip to the FBI.

The self-styled mercenaries lacked any formal military experience and/or training and the majority of the crew had been misled into joining the disastrous adventure by the ringleader, Mike Perdue, who was a con man.

White supremacist Don Black was also jailed for his part in the attempt which violated neutrality laws of the United States.

The book, *Bayou of Pigs*, written by Stewart Bell, provides details of this misguided attempt to turn Dominica into a haven for criminals and white racists.

By the end of the 1980s, the economy of Dominica had recovered. But it was weakened again in the 1990s because of a decrease in banana prices.

In the January 2000 elections, the United Workers Party (UWP) under the leadership of Edison James was defeated by the Dominican Labour Party (DLP) led by Roosevelt P. "Rosie" Douglas.

Douglas died after only a few months in office. He was replaced by Pierre Charles who also died in office in January 2004. Roosevelt Skerrit, also of the DLP, replaced Charles as prime minister.

Under Prime Minister Skerrit's leadership, the DLP won elections in May 2005.

Geography and climate

Dominica is the largest and northernmost of the Windward Islands. It's located about halfway between Puerto Rico and Trinidad and Tobago.

Oblong-shaped, the island is about four times the size of Washington, D.C. in terms of area, not population. It's slightly smaller than New York City also in terms of area.

The nation's capital, Roseau, is also the main port, favourably located on the sheltered, southwestern coast.

Dominica's nearest neighbours are the French islands of Guadeloupe located about 30 miles north, and Martinique about 25 miles south.

Geographically, Dominica is distinctive in many ways. The country has one of the most rugged landscapes in the Caribbean, covered by a largely unexploited, multi-layered rain forest.

It's also among the world's most rain-drenched lands, and the water runoff forms cascading rivers and natural pools.

The island, home to rare species of wildlife, is considered by many as a beautiful, unspoiled tropical preserve. According to a popular West Indian belief, Dominica is the only New World territory that Columbus would still recognise.

Dominica is largely covered by rain forest and is home to the world's second-largest boiling lake. It has many waterfalls, springs, and rivers. The Calibishie area in the country's northeast has sandy beaches.

Some plants and animals thought to be extinct on surrounding islands can still be found in Dominica's forests.

The volcanic nature of the island has attracted scuba divers through the years and continues to do so.

The island has several protected areas including

Cabrits National Park and 365 rivers.

Morne Trois Pitons National Park is a tropical forest blended with scenic volcanic features. It was recognised as a World Heritage Site on 4 April 1995, a distinction it shares with four other Caribbean islands.

The Commonwealth of Dominica is engaged in a long-running dispute with Venezuela over Venezuela's territorial claims to the sea surrounding Isla Aves which literally means Bird Island but called Bird Rock by Dominica authorities. It's a tiny islet located 140 miles west of the island of Dominica.

There are two primary population centres in Dominica: Roseau and Portsmouth.

Dominica has some of the most pristine wilderness in the Caribbean. Originally, it was protected by sheer mountains which led the European powers to build ports and agricultural settlements on other islands. More recently, the citizens of the island have sought to preserve its spectacular natural beauty by discouraging the type of high-impact tourism which has damaged nature in most of the Caribbean.

Visitors can find large tropical forests, hundreds of streams, coastlines and coral reefs.

The Sisserou parrot is Dominica's national bird and is indigenous to the island's mountain forests. It's on the national flag.

Dominica is especially vulnerable to hurricanes. The island is located in what is referred to as the hurricane region.

In 1979, Dominica was hit directly by category 5 Hurricane David which caused widespread and extreme damage.

On 17 August 2007, Hurricane Dean, a category 1 at the time, hit the island. A mother and her seven-year-old son died when a landslide caused by heavy rains fell on their house. In another incident two people were injured when a tree fell on their house. Prime Minister Roosevelt

Skerrit estimated that 100 to 125 homes were damaged, and that the agriculture sector was extensively damaged, especially the banana crop.

The island's hot tropical climate is moderated by heavy rainfall. It's also humid.

Excessive heat and humidity are tempered somewhat by a steady flow of the northeast trade winds which periodically develop into hurricanes.

The steep interior slopes also affect temperatures and winds. Temperature ranges are slight. Average daytime temperatures generally vary from 78.8°F in January to 89.6°F in June.

Diurnal ranges are usually no greater than 5.4°F in most places. But temperatures dipping to 55.4°F on the highest peaks are not uncommon.

Most of the island's ample supply of water is brought by the trade winds. Although amounts vary with the location, rain is possible throughout the year, with the greatest monthly totals recorded from June through October.

Average yearly rainfall along the windward east coast frequently exceeds 196.9 inches. Exposed mountainsides receive up to 354.3 inches, among the highest accumulations in the world. However, totals on the leeward west coast are only about 70.9 inches per year. Humidities are closely tied to rainfall patterns, with the highest values occurring on windward slopes and the lowest in sheltered areas. Relative humidity readings between 70 percent and 90 percent have been recorded in the nation's capital Roseau.

Hurricanes and severe winds, most likely to occur during the wettest months, occasionally are devastating. Hurricane David and Hurricane Frederic hit the island in August 1979, and Hurricane Allen in August 1980.

The 1979 hurricanes caused more than 40 deaths, 2,500 injuries, and extensive destruction of housing and crops.

Also, many agricultural commodities were destroyed during the 1980 storm. And about 25 per cent of the banana crop was destroyed by strong winds in 1984.

And in 2007, Hurricane Dean caused significant damage to the agricultural sector as well as the country's infrastructure, especially roads.

The island's natural resources include agricultural products, hydropower and timber.

Government and administrative divisions

Dominica is a parliamentary democracy and a member of the Commonwealth of Nations, an association of former British colonies. And since 1979, the island nation also has been a member of La Francophonie, an association of French-speaking countries.

And unlike the majority of countries in the Caribbean, the Commonwealth of Dominica is one of the region's few republics. The president is the head of state while executive power rests with the cabinet headed by the prime minister.

Also, unlike other former British colonies in the region which were led by prime ministers after emerging from colonial rule, Dominica was never a Commonwealth realm but instead became a republic right away on independence day headed by the island's first president.

Economy

Agriculture is Dominica's economic mainstay, and bananas its main crop.

Banana production employs directly or indirectly about one-third of the labour force. But the sector is highly vulnerable to weather conditions and to external events affecting commodity prices.

The value of banana exports fell to less than 25% of merchandise trade earnings in 1998 compared to about

44% in 1994.

In view of the European Union's announced phase-out of preferred access of bananas to its markets, agricultural diversification is a priority.

Dominica has made some progress in diversifying its agricultural production with the export of small quantities of citrus fruits and vegetables and the introduction of coffee, patchouli, aloe vera, cut flowers, and exotic fruits such as mangoes, guavas, and papayas. The country has also had some success in increasing its manufactured exports, with soap as the primary product. Dominica also recently entered the offshore financial services market.

Because the country is mostly volcanic and has few beaches, development of tourism has been slow compared with that on neighbouring islands.

Nevertheless, Dominica's high, rugged mountains, rain forests, freshwater lakes, hot springs, waterfalls, and diving spots make it an attractive destination.

Cruise ship stopovers have increased following the development of modern docking and waterfront facilities in the capital. Eco-tourism also is a growing industry on the island.

In 2008, Dominica had one of the lowest per capita gross domestic product (GDP) rates of Eastern Caribbean states.

Because Dominica is mostly volcanic and has few beaches, it has had a lot of problems in trying to develop its tourism industry. Tourism has developed more slowly than on neighbouring islands. Nevertheless, Dominica's mountains, rain forests, freshwater lakes, hot springs, waterfalls, and diving spots make it an attractive eco-tourism destination.

Cruise ship stopovers have increased following the development of modern docking and waterfront facilities in Roseau, the capital. Out of 22 Caribbean islands tracked, Dominica had the fewest visitors in 2008 (55,800 or 0.3% of the total). This was about half as many as visited Haiti.

Dominica's currency is the East Caribbean Dollar.

Dominica is a beneficiary of the U.S. Caribbean Basin Initiative that grants duty-free entry into the United States for many goods. Dominica also belongs to the predominantly English-speaking Caribbean Community (CARICOM), the CARICOM Single market and Economy (CSME), and the Organisation of East Caribbean States (OECS).

Dominica offers tax-free status to companies locating from abroad. It's not known how many companies benefit from the tax-free status because of the strict confidentiality the government enforces, although it's known many Internet businesses utilise Dominica for this reason.

Primary industries

Agriculture

About 22.6% of the total land area is arable. Agricultural production was on the decline even before the 1979 hurricane disaster. The production of bananas fell to 29,700 tons in 1978. As a result of Hurricane David, production hit a low of 15,700 tons in 1979. Agriculture suffered a further blow from Hurricane Allen in August 1980. However, after outside financial support began to rehabilitate the sector, production rose to 27,800 tons in 1981 and totaled 30,000 tons in 1999.

Agriculture accounts for about 20% of GDP and employs about 40% of the labor force. Agricultural exports amounted to $19.1 million in 2001.

Most crops are produced on small farms, the 9,000 owners of which are banded together in about 10 cooperatives. There are also several large farms that produce mostly bananas for export.

Other major crops are coconuts and citrus fruits which are grown in commercial quantities. Production for 1999 included coconuts, 11,000 tons; grapefruit, 21,000 tons; lemons and limes, 1,000 tons; and oranges, 8,000 tons. Fruits and vegetables are produced mostly for local consumption.

Animal husbandry

There are about 2,000 hectares (4,900 acres) of pasture land, comprising 2.7% of the total land area.

The island does not produce sufficient meat, poultry, or eggs for local consumption, making it necessary to import large amounts of animal products.

In 2001, there were an estimated 540 head of cattle, 9,700 goats, 7,600 sheep, and 5,000 hogs. Production of meat in the same year totalled 1,300 tons; and milk, 6,100 tons.

Fishing

Before Hurricane David, some 2,000 persons earned a living fishing in coastal waters, producing about 1,000 tons of fish a year and meeting only about one-third of the local demand.

The hurricane destroyed almost all of the island's 470 fishing boats. Afterwards, only about a dozen vessels could be reconstructed for use. In 2000, the catch was 1,150 tons, up from 552 tons in 1991.

There is a relatively large fishing industry in Dominica. But it's not modernised and almost exclusively serves the domestic market.

A successful experiment in fresh-water prawn farming, supported by Taiwanese aid, has produced substantial amounts of prawns for the domestic and local markets. Japan has provided support for a fish landing and processing plant in Roseau.

Forestry

Dominica has the potential for the development of a lumber industry. About 46,000 hectares (114,000 acres) are classified as forest, representing 61% of the total land area.

In 1962, Canadian experts produced a study indicating that over a 40-year period, the island could produce a yearly output of 22,000 cu m (800,000 cu ft) of lumber.

Before Hurricane David hit the island, annual output had reached about 7,500 cu m (265,000 cu ft).

There are about 280 hectares (700 acres) of government land allocated to commercial forestry and about 100 hectares (240 acres) of forestland in private hands.

Commercially valuable woods include mahogany, blue and red mahoe, and teak.

Total imports of forest products in 2000 amounted to $10.3 million.

Mining

Dominica's mining sector plays only a minor role in the island's economy. Pumice is the major commodity extracted from the island for export, and Dominica produces clay, limestone, volcanic ash, and sand and gravel, primarily for the construction industry.

But there is some mining potential in the country, especially in the island's northeastern part where there are believed to be deposits of copper.

Secondary industries

Dominica's small manufacturing sector is almost entirely dependent on agriculture. The island has built a few successful industries specialising in the production of soap and agricultural byproducts.

The largest manufacturer is Dominica Coconut Products owned by Colgate-Palmolive which produces soap from coconuts.

The factory has an agreement to sell an estimated 3 million bars of soap to Royal Caribbean Cruise Lines every year. Dominican soap is also exported throughout the region but has recently encountered great competition from other regional producers, especially in the important export markets of Jamaica and Trinidad and Tobago.

There are four plants to process limes and other citrus fruits; two bottling plants; two distilleries; four small apparel plants; and four small furniture factories.

Dominica exports water to its Caribbean neighbours. Shoes, cement blocks, furniture, and soap and toiletries are also exported. Also some industries produce leather work, ceramics, and straw products.

Since the 1990s, the small manufacturing sector has been expanding at a modest pace, including electronic assembly, rum, candles, and paints.

The Trafalgar Hydro Electric Power Station is now operational, making the island virtually energy self-sufficient.

Industry accounted for 23% of GDP in 2001.

Dominica has not yet been able to attract significant numbers of foreign manufacturers, partly because its wage rates are relatively high and partly because its infrastructure is not suited to high-volume manufacturing.

Like other islands, it seeks to attract investors with tax concessions and other financial inducements, but several offshore manufacturing plants have closed after their duty-free concessions expired, normally a 10-year span.

Tertiary industries

Tourism

Tourism in Dominica is mostly based on hiking in the rain forest and visiting cruise ships.

Dominica's tourism industry is still in its infancy compared to other Caribbean islands.

For many years its rugged terrain, lack of white beaches, and underdeveloped infrastructure prevented large-scale tourist development.

In recent years, Dominica has successfully marketed itself as the "nature island of the Caribbean," seeking to attract eco-tourists interested in landscapes and wildlife.

The government realises that intensive tourism is incompatible with preserving the island's eco-system and in 1997 signed an agreement with Green Globe, the environmental division of the World Travel and Tourism Council, to develop the island as a "model ecotourism destination."

The 3-year programme provided technical expertise on environmental management and helped to market Dominica through specialist travel companies and agencies.

At the same time, the government has encouraged a steady increase in Dominica's tourism capacity, with a number of new hotels being built and considerable investment being made in cruise ship facilities.

The new cruise ship jetty at Prince Rupert Bay, near Portsmouth, has dramatically increased the number of ships calling annually and has brought significant tourism-related opportunities to the formerly depressed community of Portsmouth.

Annual tourist arrivals are estimated at approximately 200,000, of whom about 75,000 are stay-over visitors. The great majority are cruise ship visitors who spend limited time and money on the island. Revenues from tourism reached US$49 million in 1999.

Compared to many other Caribbean islands, Dominica's tourism industry may be considered to be underdeveloped (about 56,000 visitors per year). And it does not have any world-famous hotels.

However, Dominica has a few famous tourist spots such as the Indian River in Portsmouth; Emerald Pool; Trafalgar Falls; Scotts Head where the Atlantic Ocean meets the Caribbean Sea; and the world's second-largest boiling lake which is inside Morne Trois Pitons National Park.

An article in *The New York Times* in 2005 stated that locals, who believe an earthquake to be the most likely culprit, claim the boiling lake had diminished in volume and effect in recent years.

Dominica also has many excellent diving spots due to its steep drop-offs, healthy marine environment, and reefs.

In 2004, because of its natural beauty, Dominica was chosen to be one of the primary filming locations for *Pirates of the Caribbean: Dead Man's Chest* and its follow-up, *At World's End*.

Hampstead Beach, Indian River, Londonderry River, Soufriere, and Vieille Case which is located on the island's northern tip, were among the places selected for filming. The production ended on 26 May 2005. And the cast and crew and their island hosts had a "Dominica Survivor Party."

Celebrity Cruises, Carnival Cruise Lines, Princess Cruise Lines, and Oceania Cruise Lines have made Dominica one of their ports of call. The pier is located in the capital city of Roseau and is a simple pier. Other Caribbean islands -- such as St. Thomas, Barbados, St. Lucia, and Antigua -- have more extensive cruise pier facilities.

The Dominica straw markets open on Tuesdays when

the cruise ship docks. These shops are operated by locals and are located on the main street directly in front of the pier, and directly behind the Dominica Museum. No other straw markets are located on the northern side of the island.

Financial services

Dominica has tried to broaden its economic base by building up an offshore financial services sector. So far, a relatively small number of offshore banks and other international business companies have registered in Dominica, but the government is trying to attract more by making registration economical and easy.

The government has also granted operating licences to several Internet gambling companies. The ease with which such companies can be formed and the secrecy surrounding their operations have led some critics to allege that Dominica may be facilitating money-laundering and tax evasion.

Demographics

Almost all Dominicans are descendants of African slaves brought in by colonial planters in the 1700s.

The population growth rate is very low mainly because of emigration. Many Dominicans have migrated and continue to migrate to more prosperous Caribbean Islands and to the United Kingdom, the United States, and Canada. Some also migrate to France because of historical ties between the two countries before the British took over the island.

English is the official language and is spoken throughout the island. But a French patois, Antillean Creole, is also widely spoken because France once controlled the island.

France occupied Dominica at different times. Also, the

island's location between the French territories of Martinique and Guadeloupe, which use the French language, has further facilitated the spread of French-based Antillean Creole on Dominica.

But Antillean Creole is spoken mainly by members of the older generation on the island of Dominica. And because of a decline in its usage by the younger generation, initiatives have been introduced in an effort to increase usage of the language and save this unique part of the nation's history and culture.

Besides French-based patois or Creole, another dialect known as Cocoy is also spoken in Dominica. Also known as Kockoy, it's a mixture of Leeward Island English-Creole and Dominican Creole. It's mainly spoken in the northeastern villages of Marigot and Wesley.

As a result of this admixture of languages and heritage, Dominica is a member of both the English-speaking Commonwealth and the French-speaking community or group known as La Francophonie.

At the beginning of the twentieth century, the Rose's Company which produced Rose's lime juice saw the demand for its product surpass its ability to supply the product from the island of Montserrat.

The company's response to the situation was to buy land on Dominica and encourage farm labourers in Montserrat relocate.

Many of them moved from Montserrat to Dominica. As a result of that, another cultural community evolved in Dominica, tracing its origin to Montserrat. But through the years, there has been much intermarrying, although there are still traces of difference in origin.

About 80 per cent of the population of Dominica is Catholic mainly because of early French influence on the island. But in recent years, a number of Protestant churches have been established.

There is also a small Muslim community in Dominica. The nation's first mosque was built recently near Ross

University.

The island also has a significant mixed minority. There are other minority groups including Indo-Caribbean or East Indian; descendants of French, British, and Irish colonists; and small numbers of Lebanese, Syrians and Asians.

Dominica also is the only island in its region which still has a population of pre-Columbian native Caribs who were exterminated or driven from neighbouring islands. There are only about 3,000 Caribs on the island. They live in eight villages on the east coast of Dominica. This special Carib Territory was granted by the British Crown in 1903.

There are also about 1,000 medical students from the United States and Canada who study at the Ross University School of Medicine in Portsmouth.

Dominica also has a relatively large number of centenarians. As of March 2007, there are 22 centenarians out of the island's 70,000 inhabitants – three times the average incidence of centenarianism in developed countries. The reasons for this are the subject of current research being undertaken at Ross University School of Medicine.

Culture

Dominica is home to a wide range of people and cultures including the indigenous Carib. But the dominant group is of African origin with its African cultural influence spread across the spectrum.

African language, foods and customs mingle with European traditions as part of the island's Creole culture. And Caribs still carve dugout canoes, build houses on stilts, and weave distinctive basketwork.

Rastafarian and Black pride influences are also common.

The Bahá'í Faith community is about 1 per cent of the

population. But it has made its presence known in the cultural milieu of Dominica.

With an almost 80 per cent Roman Catholic population, conservative traditional values are strong.

Family holds a very important place in the Dominican society, so much so that a government poster warning Dominicans of the dangers of transporting illegal drugs lists separation from family – followed by imprisonment and loss of life – as the number one deterrent to the crime.

The island's food is also a product of many cultures.

Dominican cuisine is similar to that of other Caribbean countries. Common main courses comprise meat – usually chicken, but can be goat, lamb, or beef – covered in sauce. The sauces are either spicy pepper sauces, or concoctions made from local fruit.

A wide variety of local fruit, from tamarind to passion fruit, are served usually in juice or sauce form.

Soursop is peeled and eaten raw.

Sorrel, a red flower that only blooms around Christmas, is boiled into a bright red drink.

Carnival

Each year, Dominicans celebrate the Catholic Carnival, a festival held for three days before Ash Wednesday.

Although the majority of the people are Catholic because of French heritage, many non-Catholics also celebrate the Catholic Carnival. Activities include the Calypso Monarch Competition, Carnival Queen Pageant, and Carnival parades and parties.

Music

Music and dance are important facets of Dominica's culture.

The annual independence celebrations show an

outburst of traditional song and dance preceded since 1997 by weeks of Creole expressions such as "Creole in the Park" and the "World Creole Music Festival."

Dominica gained prominence on the international music stage when, in 1973, Gordon Henderson founded the group Exile One and an original musical genre which he named "Cadence-lypso," paving the way for modern Creole music.

The 11th annual World Creole Music Festival was the first activity held in Dominica since its completion on October 27, 2007, as part of the island's celebration of independence from Great Britain on November 3. A year-long reunion celebration began in January 2008 marking 30 years of independence.

The music of Dominica plays an important role in the social and culture life of this Antillean island.

Popular music is widespread, with a number of native Dominican performers gaining national fame in imported genres such as calypso, reggae, soca, Kompa, zouk and rock and roll.

In addition to that, Dominica's own popular music industry has created a form called *bouyon* which combines elements from several styles and has achieved a wide fanbase in Dominica. The most well-known group in Dominica playing this kind of music is *WCK* (Windward Caribbean Kulture).

Native musicians in various forms have also become stars at home and abroad. They include Nasio Fontaine, Lazo, and Brother Matthew Luke playing reggae; Derick St.Rose-De Hunter, and Young Bull playing soca; Ophelia Marie playing zouk; Exile One, and Grammacks playing Cadence-Lypso; and The Wizzard, and Levi "Super L" Loblack & Michele Henderson playing calypso.

Like the other Francophone music of the Lesser Antilles, Dominican folk music is a hybrid of African and European elements.

The quadrille is an important symbol of French

Antillean culture and is – n on the island of Dominica – typically accompanied by a kind of ensemble called a *jing ping* band.

In addition too all that, Dominica's folk tradition includes folk songs called *bélé*, traditional storytelling called *kont*, masquerade, children's and work songs, and Carnival music.

Until the late 1950s, the Afro-Dominican culture of most of the island was repressed by the colonial government and by the influence of the Roman Catholic Church. Both taught that African-derived music was evil, demonic and uncultured. This perception changed in the mid- to late 20th century when Afro-Dominican culture came to be celebrated through the work of promoters such as Cissie Caudeiron.

Characteristics of Dominican music

Dominica's rugged terrain rugged has fostered distinct regional traditions.

The northern, eastern, southern, western and central parts of the island are all music areas but sometimes with regional variation.

The villages of Wesley and Marigot are also unique in their preservation of the English language and music rather than the more French-based styles of the rest of the island.

Dominican folk music is a product of oral tradition, and is an oral tradition itself, learned informally through watching others perform.

As of 1987, most performers of traditional music were either over 50 years old or under 35, which indicates an ongoing revival of previously declining traditions.

Music evaluation is based on the characteristics of the music such as complex syncopated rhythms and on social factors such as the ability of the performers to improvise and respond to their surroundings and to keep the audience excited and participate in the music.

Characteristics of Dominican music include the West African use of call and response singing, clapping as a major part of rhythm and dance and lyrical and rhythmic improvisation.

Almost all lyrics are in French Creole and are traditionally sung by women (*chantwèl*), while the instrumental traditions are predominantly practised by men.

Drums, generically known as *lapo kabwit*, are the most prominent part of Dominica's instrumental tradition.

Folk music

Dominican folk music includes, most influentially, the French Antillean quadrille tradition, the *jing ping* style of dance music, as well as *bélé* and heel-and-toe polka.

Traditional carnival music includes *chante mas* and *lapo kabwit*. Folk music on Dominica has historically been a part of everyday life including work songs, religious music and secular, recreational music.

The quadrille is one of the most important dances of the Dominican folk tradition which also includes the lancer and distinctive forms of several dances, many of them derived from European styles.

The *bidjin* (biguine), *mereng* (merengue), *sotis* (schottische), *polka pil* (pure polka), *vals o vyenn* (Viennese waltz) and *mazouk* (mazurka) are particularly widespread.

Bélé

Belé are folk songs of West African origin, traditionally performed for recreation in the evening during the full moon and, more rarely, *lavèyé* (wakes).

The bélé tradition has declined in the 20th and 21st century but is still performed for holidays like Easter,

Independence Day, Christmas, Jounen Kweyol, and patron saint festivals held annually in the Parishes of Dominica especially in the *Fèt St.-Pierre* and the *Fèt St.-Isidore* for fishermen and workers respectively.

All bélé are accompanied by an eponymous drum, the *tanbou bélé* along with the *tingting* (triangle) and *chakchak* (maracas).

Bélés start with a lead vocalist who is followed by chorus (*lavwa*) in response, then a drummer and dancers.

Traditional dances revolve around stylized courtship between a male and female dancer known as the *kavalyé* and *danm* respectively.

The bélé song-dances include the *bélé soté*, *bélé priòrité*, *bélé djouba*, *bélé contredanse*, *bélé rickety* and *bélé pitjé*.

Quadrille

The quadrille is a dance form that is an important symbol of French Antillean culture, not just in Dominica, but also in Martinique, Guadeloupe and other Francophone islands.

Dominican quadrilles are traditionally performed by four sets of couples in subscription picnics or dances and in private parties. However, the quadrille tradition now only survives at holidays and festivals.

The Dominican quadrille generally has four figures: the *pastouwèl*, *lapoul*, *lété* and *latrinitez*.

Some regions of Dominica such as Petite Savanne are home to local variants, for example, the *caristo*.

Many quadrilles are found across Dominica under a wide variety of names.

In addition to the standard quadrille, the lancer is also an important Dominican dance.

Accompaniment for the quadrille is provided by a four instrument ensemble called a *jing ping* band or, less commonly, an *accordion band*. Jing ping groups also accompany the *flirtation*, a circle dance.

Jing ping bands are made up of a *boumboum* (boom pipe), *syak* or *gwaj* (scraper-rattle), *tambal* or *tanbou* (tambourine) and accordion.

The double bass and banjo are also sometimes used.

Bamboo flutes led the jing ping ensembles before the 1940s when accordions were introduced. The Dominican flute tradition declined as a result, despite the additional use of flutes in serenades. But the flute tradition was revived after the National Independence Competitions.

Other folk music

Dominica's folk musical heritage includes work songs, storytelling children's music and masquerade songs.

Work songs are accompanied by the *tambou twavay* drum and are performed by workers while gathering fruit, building roads, fishing, moving a house or sawing wood. Many are short and simple, with the lyrical text and rhythm tying into the work to be accompanied. But work songs are rarely performed in Dominica today.

The *kont*, or storytelling, folk tradition of Dominica was focused on entertainment for night-time festivals, funeral wakes and feasts and festivals. Modern *kont* is mostly performed during major festival competitions.

Most *kont* storytellers work with local traditions such as legends and history and provide an ethical or moral message. A one line theme song, often weaved around a duet between two characters, recurs throughout most *kont* performances.

Unlike most Dominican folk songs, children's songs and musical games are mostly in English. They were originally in the same Creole language as the rest on the island but have come to be primarily of English, Scottish, and Irish derivation.

Children's musical traditions include ring games and circle dances, and music accompanied by thigh-slapping and circle dancing.

The chanté mas (masquerade song) tradition is based on pre-calypso carnival music performed in a responding style by partygoers.

Traditionally, the Dominican carnival masquerade lasted for two days of parading through the streets, with a singer dancing backwards in front of the drummer on a *tanbou lélé*. Chanté mas lyrics were traditionally based on gossip and scandal and addressed the personal shortcomings of others.

Popular music

The first internationally known bands from Dominica were Exile One and Grammacks and others like them in the 1970s. These bands were the stars of the cadence-lypso scene which was the first style of Dominican music to become popular across the Caribbean.

By the 1980s, however, Martinican zoukn and other styles were more popular. In 1988, WCK was started, playing an experimental fusion of cadence-lypso with the island's jing ping sound. The result came to be known as bouyon, a music style which has re-established Dominica in the field of popular music.

Early popular music

Dominican popular music history can be traced back to the 1940s and 50s when dance bands like the Casimir Brothers and later, The swinging Stars, became famous across the island.

Their music was a dance-oriented version of many kinds of Caribbean and Latin popular music such as Cuban bolero, Brazilian samba, merengue of the Dominican Republic and Trinidadian calypso and funk.

By the beginning of the 1960s, calypso and Trinidadian steelpan became the most popular styles of music on

Dominica island, replacing traditional carnival music like chanté mas and lapo kabwit.

Early recording stars from this era included Swinging Busters, The Gaylords, De Boys an Dem, and Los Caballeros, while chorale groups also gained fans, especially Lajenne Etwal, Sifle Montan'y and the Dominica Folk singers.

These early popular musicians were helped by the spread of radio broadcasting, starting with WIDBS and later Radio Dominica.

Of these early popular musicians, a few pioneered the use of native influences.

The Gaylords' hits like "Ti Mako", "Pray for the Blackman", "Lovely Dominica," and "Douvan Jo" were either in English or the native Creole, *kwéyòl*.

By the end of the 1960s and beginning of the 1970s, American rock and roll, soul and funk had reached Dominica and left lasting influences. Funky rock-based bands lsuch as Voltage Four, Woodenstool, and Every Mother's Child became popular.

Calypso has been popular in Dominica since the 1950s. The first Calypso King was crowned in 1959. Popular calypso in Dominica has always been closely associated with steelpan music. The first wave of Dominican steelpan includes bands such as Esso, Shell and Regent, Vauxhall, and Old Oak.

Cadence-lypso was developed in the 1970s and was the first style of Dominican music to find international acclaim, eventually becoming a part of styles like zouk. The most influential band in the development of cadence-lypso was Exile One who combined cadence-rampa with calypso.

Cadence-lypso was influenced by the nationalist movement which espoused Rastafari and Black Power. Many groups performed songs with intensely ideological positions, and much of the repertoire was in the vernacular *kwéyòl* language.

Recent popular music

During the 1980s, cadence-lypso's popularity declined greatly. Some Dominican performers remained famous, such as Ophelia, a very renowned singer of the period.

Popular music during that period was mostly zouk, a style pioneered by the Martinican band Kassay who used styles of the folk music of Martinique and Guadeloupe.

Soca, a kind of Trinidadian music, was also popular at the time, producing bands such as RSB, Windward Caribbean Kulture (WCK) and Firsk Serenade.

The 80s also saw a rise in popularity for jazz and the formation of several jazz bands, while groups such as Exile One began exploring traditional rhythms from *jing ping* and *lapo kabwit*.

Another recent form of popular music, bouyon, is a fusion of jing ping, cadence-lypso and other styles of Caribbean music developed by a band called *Windward Caribbean Kulture* (later *WCK*).

WCK was one of the most prominent soca bands in Dominica and in the entire Caribbean in the 1980s. They began using native drum rhythms and elements of the music of jing ping bands as well as raggar-style vocals.

Bouyon is popular across the Caribbean and is known as *jump up music* in Guadeloupe and Martinique.

A modern offshoot of bouyon, bouyon-muffin, uses more prominent elements of Jamaican raggamuffin music. Modern bouyon bands include Rough and Ready, Wassin Warriors, and Seramix.

Reketeng is a form of Dub music from Dominica. It's linked to Bouyon-muffin as sung by Skinny Banton.

The term *Reketeng* is a written slang for *wreck a teng*. Bushtown Clan originated the style in 1999 by doing remixes of existing hip-hop and dancehall songs over bouyon rhythms.

Religious music, influenced by American gospel, has

become an important part of Dominican popular music in the 1990s. Performers include Cegid, Exeters, Agnes Aaron, Leon Esprit, Jerry Lloyd and End Time Singers.

Calypso has also retained much popularity on the island of Dominica as has jazz. The band Impact has fused jazz with Caribbean music.

Steelpan has declined in popularity on the island despite efforts by groups such as Phase Five, and dancehall which includes performers like Puppa Tino, Miekey Moereau, Cecil Moses and Skinny Banton, to sustain it.

Music institutions and festivals

The Caribbean carnival is an important part of Dominican culture.

Originally featuring masquerade songs (*chanté mas*) and other local traditions, the traditional carnival, *Mas Domnik*, came to be dominated by imported calypso music and steel bands in the early 1960s.

Calypso appealed to carnival-goers because the lyrical focus on local news and gossip was similar to that of *chanté mas* despite a rhythmic pattern and instrumentation which contrast sharply with traditional Dominican *Mas Domnik* music.

After a fire in 1963, the traditional carnival was banned, although calypso and steelpan continued to grow in popularity and influence.

The modern carnival on Dominica takes place on the Monday and Tuesday before Ash Wednesday. It's a festive occasion during which laws against libel and slander are suspended.

The modern Dominican carnival is heavily influenced by the Trinidadian carnival; but it's not as commercialised because of a lack of corporate sponsorship.

Another major musical and cultural event is The World Creole Music Festival which takes place on the island of

Dominica, in Festival City, Roseau. It's managed by the governmental Dominica Festivals Commission.

Also, the National Independence Competitions are an important part of Dominican musical culture. They were started by Chief Minister of Dominica Edward Olivier Leblanc in 1965 to promote the traditional music and dance of Dominica.

The Dominican government also promotes Dominican music through the Dominican Broadcasting Station which broadcasts between 20% and 25% local music as a matter of policy.

Religion in Dominica

About 61 percent of the people on the island of Dominica are Roman catholic.

Followers of evangelical churches constitute 18 per cent of the population, Seventh-day Adventists (SDA) 6 percent, and Methodists 3.7 percent.

Minority religious groups and denominations whose members range from 1.6 percent to 0.2 percent of the population include Rastafarians, Jehovah's Witnesses, Anglicans, and Muslims. And 1.4 percent of the population belongs to "other" religious groups including Baptist, Nazarene, Church of Christ, Brethren Christian, and the Bahá'í Faith. About 6 percent of the population claims no religious affiliation.

Education

The island of Dominica has its own state college, formerly named Clifton Dupigny Community College.

Some Dominicans get scholarships from the Cuban government to attend universities in Cuba. Others go to the University of the West Indies or to schools in the United Kingdom, the United States, or other countries for higher education.

Ross University, a medical school, is located in Portsmouth.

The Archbold Tropical Research and Education Centre, a biological field station owned by Clemson University, is located at Springfield Estate between Canefield and Pond Cassé.

In 2006, another medical school called All Saints University of Medicine opened in temporary facilities in Loubiere, with a permanent campus being constructed in Grand Bay. Currently All Saints is located in Roseau, Dominica's capital.

There is also a marine biology school, the Institute for Tropical Marine Ecology (I.T.M.E) located in Mahaut, about 15 minutes north of Roseau.

Chapter Eight:

Grenada

GRENADA is an island nation in the southeastern Caribbean Sea. It's located northwest of Trinidad and Tobago, northeast of Venezuela, and southwest of Saint Vincent and the Grenadines. It consists of the island of Grenada and six smaller islands at the southern end of the Grenadines.

Grenada is also known as the "Island of Spice" due to its production of nutmeg and mace crops of which the island nation is one of the world's largest exporters. As the "Island of Spice," Grenada shares this identity with another island, Zanzibar in East Africa, which is known as "Spice Island" because of its production of cloves for which it has won international acclaim for centuries.

Grenada has an area of 133 square miles and an estimated population of 110,000.

Its capital is St. George's.

History

Early History

Before the arrival of Europeans, Grenada was inhabited by Carib Indians who had driven the more peaceful Arawaks from the island.

Columbus first saw Grenada in 1498 during his third voyage to the New World. He named the island "Concepcion."

The origin of the name "Grenada" is obscure. But it's likely that Spanish sailors renamed the island after the city of Granada in Spain.

By the beginning of the 18th century, the name "Grenada," or "la Grenade" in French, was in common use.

The British first arrived in Grenada in 1609. But partly because of resistance by the Caribs, Grenada remained uncolonised for more than one hundred years after its discovery. Early attempts by the British – from England - to settle on the island were unsuccessful.

In 1650, a French company founded by Cardinal Richelieu purchased Grenada from the English and established a small settlement on the island. But it wasn't plain sailing for the French. They were on hostile territory, having taken the land from the indigenous people.

After several skirmishes with the Caribs, the French brought in reinforcements from Martinique and defeated the Caribs, the last of whom leaped into the sea rather than surrender.

18th century

In 1705, The French began building Fort George as Fort Royal on St George's. But they did not finish building it. The fort was completed by the British in 1710.

However, the island remained under French control until 1762 when it was captured by the British during the Seven Years' War.

Grenada was formally ceded to Britain by France under the Treaty of Paris in 1763.

But the French regained control of Grenada during the American War of Independence after they won the Battle of Grenada in July 1779. However, the island was restored to Britain under the Treaty of Versailles in 1783.

Restoration of British control of the island did not go unchallenged. Pro-French groups on the island revolted in 1795 and the British had a hard time containing the uprising. The revolt was finally suppressed and Grenada remained under British control for the remainder of the colonial period.

During the 18th century, Grenada's economy underwent an important transition. Like much of the rest of the West Indies, Grenada was originally occupied by Europeans to grow sugarcane. The sugarcane was grown on plantations using slaves from Africa.

But natural disasters paved the way for the introduction of other crops.

In 1782, Sir Joseph Banks, the botanical adviser to King George III, introduced nutmeg to Grenada. The island's soil was ideal for growing the spice and because Grenada was a closer source of spices for Europe than the Dutch East Indies, the island assumed a new importance to European traders.

19th century

The collapse of the sugar estates and the introduction of nutmeg and cocoa encouraged the development of smaller land holdings, and the island developed a land-owning yeoman farmer class.

Slavery was outlawed in 1834.

In 1833, just before slavery was to be abolished the following year, Grenada became part of the British Windward Islands Administration.

The governor of the Windward Islands administered the island for the rest of the colonial period.

On the 3rd of December 1882, the largest wooden Jetty ever built in Grenada was opened. The event took place in Gouyave.

In 1895, the 340-foot Sendall Tunnel was built for horse carriages.

20th century and independence

On September the 22nd 1955, Hurricane Janet hit Grenada and 500 people were killed. Also, 75 per cent of the nutmeg trees on the island were destroyed.

In 1958, the Windward Islands Administration was dissolved and Grenada joined the Federation of the West Indies. After the federation collapsed in 1962, the British government tried to form a small federation out of its remaining dependencies in the Eastern Caribbean but failed to do so.

Following the failure of this second effort at unification, the British and the islanders developed the concept of "associated statehood."

Under the Associated Statehood Act of 1967, Grenada was granted full autonomy over its internal affairs. It also won partial independence from Britain on the 3rd of March the same year. The island colony won full independence on 7 February 1974.

After winning independence, Grenada adopted a modified Western parliamentary system based on the British model.

The government is headed by a prime minister who is the leader of the majority party in parliament.

The head of state is the British monarch, currently

Queen Elizabeth II, who is represented by the governor-general in Grenada. The governor-general is a Grenadian.

Sir Eric Gairy was Grenada's first prime minister when the country won independence.

There were many Grenadians who were opposed to Gairy's leadership. Civil conflict gradually broke out between Eric Gairy's government and some opposition parties including the New Jewel Movement (NJM).

Gairy's party won elections in 1976 but the opposition did not accept the results, accusing it of fraudulence.

Revolution and US invasion

On 13 March 1979, the New Jewel Movement launched an armed revolution which overthrew Prime Minister Gairy, suspended the constitution, and established a People's Revolutionary Government (PRG) headed by Maurice Bishop who declared himself prime minister.

The constitution was suspended and Bishop's government ruled subsequently by decree.

Agrarian reforms started by Gairy's government continued and greatly expanded under the revolutionary government of Maurice Bishop.

Bishop's government also established close ties with Cuba, Nicaragua, and other countries including those in the communist bloc.

Cuban heavily invested in civic assistance (doctors, teachers, and technicians in the fields of health, literacy, agriculture, and agro-industries) during Bishop's leadership.

All political parties except for the New Jewel Movement were banned and no elections were held during the four years of PRG rule.

In October 1983, a power struggle within the government resulted in the arrest of Maurice Bishop on orders from his deputy prime minister, Bernard Coard.

Bishop was illegally placed under house arrest.

Bishop's removal from office resulted in demonstrations in various parts of the island which eventually led to his release from house arrest.

But he was still under restriction imposed on him by his opponents in the government. Coard's forces eventually executed him and seven others including members of his cabinet.

After Bishop's execution, the military under Hudson Austin took power and formed a military government to run the country.

A four-day total curfew was imposed on the entire island under which any civilian outside his or her home was subject to summary execution.

On 25 October 1983, an invasion force landed on the island. The invasion was codenamed Operation Urgent Fury and the invading force was composed of troops from a number of island nations in the Caribbean. It was led by the United States.

The invasion was launched in response to an appeal from the governor-general and to a request for assistance from the Organisation of Eastern Caribbean States without consulting the island's head of state, Queen Elizabeth II, Commonwealth institutions or other usual diplomatic channels as had been done in the case of Anguilla.

Furthermore, the American government under President Ronald Reagan feared that Soviet use of the island would enable the Soviet Union to project tactical military power over the entire Caribbean region. President Reagan also did not want to see any government in power which was friendly to Cuba or any other communist country.

Just before the invasion, American citizens including students at Grenada's medical school in the island's capital were evacuated from the island.

Constitutional government was re-instituted later.

Seventeen members of Maurice Bishop's People's Revolutionary Government (PRG) and the People's Revolutionary Army (PRA) were convicted of various offences and crimes.

Fourteen were sentenced to death for actions related to the overthrow of the Bishop government and the murder of several persons including Bishop. The sentences were eventually commuted to life imprisonment after an international campaign.

Another three were sentenced to 45 years in prison.

The seventeen have came to be known as the Grenada 17 and are the subject of an ongoing international campaign for their release.

After the invasion, United States gave $48.4 million in economic assistance to Grenada in 1984.

An advisory council named by the governor-general administered the country until general elections were held in December 1984. The New National Party (NNP) led by Herbert Blaize won fourteen out of fifteen seats in elections and formed a democratic government. Grenada's constitution had been suspended in 1979 by the PRG but it was restored after the 1984 elections.

Late 20th century

The New National Party continued to rule until 1989 but with a reduced majority. Five NNP parliamentary members, including two cabinet ministers, left the party in 1986-87 and formed the National Democratic Congress (NDC) which became the official opposition.

In August 1989, Prime Minister Blaize broke with the NNP to form another new party, The National Party (TNP), from the ranks of the NNP. This split in the NNP resulted in the formation of a minority government until constitutionally scheduled elections in March 1990.

Prime Minister Blaize died in December 1989 and was

succeeded as prime minister by Ben Jones until after the elections.

The NDC emerged from the 1990 elections as the strongest party, winning seven of the fifteen available seats. Nicholas Brathwaite added two TNP members and one member of the Grenada United Labor Party (GULP) to create a 10-seat majority coalition. The governor-general appointed him to be prime minister.

In parliamentary elections on June 20, 1995, the NNP won eight seats and formed a government headed by Dr. Keith Mitchell. The NNP maintained and affirmed its hold on power when it took all fifteen parliamentary seats in the January 1999 elections.

21st century

Truth and reconciliation commission

In 2000-2002, much of the controversy of the late 1970s and early 1980s was once again brought into the public consciousness with the opening of the truth and reconciliation commission.

The commission was chaired by a Catholic priest, Father Mark Haynes, and was tasked with uncovering injustices arising from the People's Revolutionary Army (PRA), Bishop's regime, and before. It held a number of hearings around the country.

The commission was formed, bizarrely, because of a school project.

Brother Robert Fanovich, head of Presentation Brothers' College (PBC) in St. George's assigned some of his senior students to conduct a research project into the era and specifically into the fact that Maurice Bishop's body was never discovered.

Their project attracted a great deal of attention. The *Miami Herald*, a newspaper in Miami in the state of

Florida in the United States, was one of the papers interested in the case, as were many individuals and a number of institutions and organisations in and outside Grenada, especially because of the assassination of Prime Minister Maurice Bishop and the invasion of the island spearheaded by the United States under President Reagan, a staunch conservative.

The final report was published in a book written by the boys called *Big Sky, Little Bullet*. It also uncovered that there was still a lot of resentment in Grenadian society resulting from the era, and a feeling that there were many injustices still not addressed. The commission began its work shortly after the boys concluded their project.

Hurricane Ivan

On 7 September 2004, after being hurricane-free for 49 years, Grenada was hit directly by Hurricane Ivan. The hurricane destroyed about 90 per cent of the structures on the island including the prison and the prime minister's residence, killed 39 people, and destroyed most of the nutmeg crop, Grenada's mainstay of the economy.

Grenada's economy was set back several years by Hurricane Ivan's impact.

After Hurricane Ivan, the government of the People's Republic of China (PRC) was one of the countries which helped to rebuild the island. Among the projects it financed was the construction of a new stadium at a cost of $40 million.

When a world cricket match was held at the stadium in 2007, the anthem of the Republic of China (Taiwan) was accidentally played instead of the PRC's anthem, leading to the firing of top officials.

Another hurricane, Emily, wreaked havoc on the island on 14 July 2005. It struck the northern part of the island with 92-mile-per-hour winds, causing an estimated USD $110 million (EC$ 297 million) worth of damage.

But the damage was much less than what Ivan had caused earlier.

The island nation has recovered with remarkable speed from the destruction caused by the two hurricanes, mainly because of the efforts by the people of Grenada themselves; also because of financial assistance from the international community.

The reconstruction effort was led by the New National Party government of Dr. Keith Mitchell.

The agricultural sector, especially the nutmeg industry, suffered serious losses. But it's hoped that as new nutmeg trees gradually mature, the industry will return to its pre-Ivan levels making Grenada once again a major supplier of nutmeg to many countries in the Western part of the world.

Invasion of Grenada by the United States and OECS military: A Closer Look

The invasion of Grenada was preceded by a dispute between socialist Prime Minister Maurice Bishop and some high-ranking members of his ruling party, the New Jewel Movement (NJM).

Although Bishop was cooperated with Cuba and the Soviet Union on various trade and foreign policy issues, he sought to maintain a "non-aligned" status in his dealings with world powers.

He wanted to transform Grenada into a socialist state. But he also encouraged private-sector development in an attempt to make the island a popular tourist destination.

Hardline Marxist party members including communist Deputy Prime Minister Bernard Coard deemed Bishop insufficiently revolutionary and demanded that he either step down or enter into a power sharing arrangement.

On 19 October 1983, Bernard Coard and his wife Phyllis, backed by the Grenadian Army, led a coup against the government of Maurice Bishop who was placed under house arrest.

These actions led to street demonstrations in various parts of the island. Bishop had massive support among the population and was eventually freed by a large demonstration in the capital.

When Bishop attempted to resume power, he was captured and executed by soldiers along with seven others, including government cabinet ministers. The Coard regime then put the island under martial law.

After the execution of Bishop, the People's Revolutionary Army (PRA) formed a military government with General Hudson Austin as chairman. The army declared a four-day total curfew during which it said that anyone leaving their home without approval would be shot on sight.

The overthrow of Prime Minister Gairy's moderate government by one which was friendly with communist countries worried U.S. President Ronald Reagan. Of particular concern was the presence of Cuban construction workers and military personnel building a 10,000-foot airport runway on Grenada.

Maurice Bishop claimed the purpose of the airstrip was to allow commercial jets to land. But Reagan believed its purpose was to allow military transport planes loaded with arms from Cuba to be transferred to Central American insurgents.

On 25 October 1983, Grenada was invaded by combined forces from the United States, the Regional Security System (RSS) and Jamaica in an operation codenamed Operation Urgent Fury.

The United States stated this was done at the behest of Prime Minister Eugenia Charles of Dominica.

While Grenada's governor-general, Sir Paul Scoon, later stated that he had also requested the invasion, it was highly criticised by the governments of the United Kingdom, Trinidad and Tobago and Canada.

The United Nations General Assembly also condemned the invasion as "a flagrant violation of international law"] by a vote of 108 to 9, with 27 abstentions. The United Nations Security Council considered a similar resolution but it failed to pass because of American opposition. It was vetoed by the United States.

After the invasion of the island nation, the pre-revolutionary Grenadian constitution was restored.

Eighteen – some reports say seventeen – members of the People's Revolutionary Government and the People's Revolutionary Army (PRA) were arrested after the invasion on charges related to the murder of Maurice Bishop and seven others.

The eighteen included the top political leadership of Grenada at the time of the execution as well as the entire military chain of command directly responsible for the operation that led to the executions.

Fourteen were sentenced to death, one was found not guilty, and three were sentenced to forty-five years in prison. The death sentences were eventually commuted to terms of imprisonment.

Geography

There are no large inland bodies of water on the island. The island is volcanic in origin and its topography/landscape is mountainous.

Natural resources include timber, tropical fruit and deep-water harbours.

Grenada and its largely uninhabited outlying territories are the most southerly of the Windward Islands.

The Grenadine Islands chain consists of some 600 islets; those south of the Martinique Channel belong to Grenada, while those north of the channel are part of the island nation of St. Vincent and the Grenadines.

About the size – in terms of area – of the city of Detroit

in the state of Michigan in the United States, the island of Grenada is oval-shaped and framed by a jagged southern coastline; its maximum width is thirty-four kilometers, and its maximum length is nineteen kilometers.

St. George's, the capital and the nation's most important harbour, is favourably located near a lagoon on the southwestern coast.

Of all the islands belonging to Grenada, only two are significant: Carriacou, with a population of a few thousand, and its neighbuor Petit Martinique, roughly 40 kilometers northeast of Grenada and populated by some 700 inhabitants.

Part of the volcanic chain in the Lesser Antilles arc, Grenada and its possessions generally vary in elevation from under 300 meters to over 600 meters above sea level.

Grenada is more rugged and densely foliated than its outlying possessions but other geographical conditions are more similar.

Grenada's landmass rises from a narrow, coastal plain in a generally north-south trending axis of ridges and narrow valleys. Mount St. Catherine is the highest peak in the country. It's 2,756 feet high.

Although many of the rocks and soils are of volcanic origin, the volcanic cones dotting Grenada are long dormant. Some of the drainage features on Grenada remain from its volcanic past.

There are a few crater lakes, the largest of which is Grand Etang.

The swift upper reaches of rivers, which occasionally overflow and cause flooding and landslides, generally cut deeply into the conic slopes. By contrast, many of the water courses in the lowlands tend to be sluggish and meandering.

The island Grenada itself is the largest island; smaller Grenadines are Carriacou, Petit Martinique, Ronde Island, Caille Island, Diamond Island, Large Island, Saline Island, and Frigate Island.

Most of the people live on Grenada itself. And besides the capital St. St. George's, other major towns on Grenada island are Grenville and Gouyave. The largest settlement on the other islands is Hillsborough on Carriacou.

The islands of Grenada have extremely rich soil because they're of volcanic origin.

Grenada's interior is very mountainous. Mount St. Catherine is on Grenada itself.

Several small rivers with beautiful waterfalls flow into the sea from the mountains.

The climate is tropical: hot and humid in the rainy season and cooled by trade winds during the dry season. Being on the southern edge of the hurricane belt, Grenada has suffered only three hurricanes in fifty years.

Hurricane Janet passed over Grenada on Friday 23 September 1955 with winds of 115 miles per hour, causing severe damage.

The most recent storms to hit have been Hurricane Ivan on Tuesday 7 September 2004 causing severe damage and thirty-nine deaths; and Hurricane Emily on Thursday 14 July 2005, causing serious damage in Carriacou and in the northern part of the island of Grenada which had been lightly affected by Hurricane Ivan.

Climate

Grenada has a lot of water, in sharp contrast with the Cayman Islands, for example, another island nation in the Caribbean.

The abundance of water in Grenada is primarily caused by the tropical, wet climate.

The greatest monthly precipitation are recorded throughout Grenada from June to November, the months when tropical storms and hurricanes are most likely to occur. Rainfall is less pronounced from December through May when the equatorial low-pressure system moves south.

Similarly, the highest humidities, usually close to 80 per cent, are recorded during the rainy months, and values from 68 to 78 per cent are registered during the drier period.

Temperatures averaging 84.2°F are constant throughout the year, with slightly higher readings in the lowlands. Nevertheless, diurnal ranges within a 24-hour period are appreciable: between 78.8 and 89.6°F during the day, and between 66.2 and 75.2°F at night.

Politics

Grenada has a parliamentary system. The prime minister is the head of government. Its political and legal traditions closely follow those of the United Kingdom, its former colonial ruler.

Queen Elizabeth II is the head of state.

Economy and tourism

Grenada has a largely tourism-based economy.

Since the early 1990s, the economy has shifted from agriculture to being mainly service-oriented. Tourism is the leading foreign currency earning sector.

However, agriculture remains a major sector of the economy. The country's principal export crops are spices: nutmeg and mace. Grenada is the world's second-largest producer of nutmeg after Indonesia.

Other crops for export include cocoa, citrus fruits, bananas, cloves, and cinnamon.

Manufacturing industries operate mostly on a small scale. They include the production of beverages and other foodstuffs. Grenada also manufactures textiles. It also assembles electronic components for export.

Economic growth picked up in the late 1990s

following slow growth and domestic fiscal adjustment in the early years of the decade.

Since 2001, economic growth declined caused by adverse shocks such as a slowdown in the global economy and natural disasters.

Economic conditions worsened when Hurricane Ivan hit the country in September 2004. And progress in fiscal consolidation was impeded as government revenues fell and policy priority was shifted to post-hurricane relief.

Although reconstruction has proceeded quickly with significant aid from the international community, tourism and agricultural activities remain weak and nearly offset the stimulus from the reconstruction boom.

The country is still facing the difficult task of reconstruction and recovery, while public debt is unsustainable and the government faces large financing gaps.

In the years ahead, reinvigorating growth will be a high priority, and continued efforts are needed to address vulnerabilities.

Economic Performance

After experiencing GDP growth averaging nearly six percent a year in the late 1990s, economic growth declined considerably after 2001 as a result of a decline in the tourism industry following the September 11, 2001, terrorist attacks, and damages caused by several hurricanes.

The economy of Grenada was brought to a near standstill in September 2004 by Hurricane Ivan, which damaged or destroyed 90 percent of the country's buildings, including some tourist facilities.

In July 2005, Hurricane Emily struck Grenada again as the country was still recovering from the impact of Hurricane Ivan.

Besides the negative impacts to the tourism industry, the two devastating hurricanes destroyed or significantly damaged a large percentage of Grenada's tree crops, which may take years to recover.

Although signs of recovery have been seen in Grenada after the damage inflicted by Hurricanes Ivan and Emily, economic conditions remain difficult.

Grenada's economy is vulnerable to external shocks considering its high dependence on tourism, exports, and imports of most of the goods that are consumed or invested domestically. It's also prone to other adverse shocks such as natural disasters.

Grenada is a member of the Eastern Caribbean Central Bank (ECCB) which manages monetary policy and issues a common currency for all the member countries. The currency is the East Caribbean dollar shared by the seven members of the Organisation of Eastern Caribbean States (OECS).

Grenada is called **The Spice Isle** because it is a leading producer of several different spices. Cinnamon, cloves, ginger, mace, allspice, orange/citrus peels, wild coffee used by the locals, and especially nutmeg, providing 20% of the world supply, are all important exports.

The nutmeg on the nation's flag represents the nation's leading economic crop of Grenada.

As the country main economic sector, tourism is getting a lot of attention in order to improve it and fuel economic growth.

Conventional beach and water-sports tourism is largely focused in the southwestern region around St Georges, the airport and the coastal strip. However, ecotourism is growing in significance.

Most of the small eco-friendly guest houses are located in the Saint David and Saint John parishes. You will find a lot of different accommodations ranging from luxurious ones such as the Spice Island Beach Resort to small cottages resorts like Mango Beach Cottages.

The tourism industry is increasing dramatically with the construction of a large cruise ship pier and esplanade. Up to 4 cruise ships per day were visiting St. Georges in 2007–8 during the cruise ship season.

The island has also pioneered the cultivation of organic cocoa which is also processed into finished bars by the Grenada Chocolate Company.

Tourism is concentrated in the southwestern part of the island of Grenada around the capital St. Georges, Grand Anse, Lance Aux Epines, and Point Salines.

Grenada has many idyllic beaches around its coastline including the 1.9-mile long Grand Anse Beach in St. George's which is considered to be one of the finest beaches in the world, and often appears in countdowns of the world's top 10 beaches.

Grenada is linked to the world through the Maurice Bishop International Airport and the St. George's harbour. International flights connect with other Caribbean islands, the United States, and Europe.

There is also a daily fast ferry service between St. George's and Hillsborough.

And in October, 2009, a new passenger ferry service between Grenada, Barbados, St. Vincent, St. Lucia, and Trinidad provided by Grenada-based BEDY Ocean Line was scheduled to begin during that time.

Demographics

A vast majority of the people of Grenada are descendants of the African slaves taken to the islands by the English and French. Few of the indigenous Carib and Arawak population survived the French purge at Sauteurs.

Descendants of East Indian indentured workers who were taken to Grenada mainly from the North Indian states of Bihar and Uttar Pradesh between 1 May 1857 and 10 January 1885 constitute a small minority. There is also a small community of French and English descendants.

The rest of the population is of mixed descent.

Like most of the Caribbean islands, Grenada is a source of a large number of emigrants, especially young people wanting to leave the island in search of better life elsewhere.

With just 110,000 people living in Grenada, estimates and census data suggest that there are at least just as many Grenadian-born people in other parts of the Caribbean such as Barbados and Trinidad, and at least that number in Western countries as well.

Popular destinations include New York City and other parts of the United States; Toronto as well as other parts of Canada such as Montreal in Quebec; the United Kingdom, especially London and Yorkshire; and even Australia. This means that probably around a third of those born in Grenada still live there.

Although English is the official language of Grenada, the vast majority of the people also speak Grenadian Creole which is considered the lingua franca of the island. Another form of Creole, French Patois which is also known as Antillean Creole, is spoken by about 10%–20% the population.

French patois links Grenada to France but a more significant reminder of Grenada's historical link with France is the strength of the Roman Catholic Church on the island. The majority of Grenadians are Catholic.

Among the descendants of East Indians, some Hindi/Bhojpuri terms – mostly those pertaining to the kitchen – are still used; terms such as *aloo, geera, karela, seim, chownkay, and baylay.*

The term *bhai*, which means "brother" or "partner" in Hindi, is a common form of greeting amongst Indo-Grenadian males of equal status.

Religion

Apart from a marginal community of Rastafarians in Grenada, nearly all of the population belong to Christian churches.

About half of the population are Roman Catholics. The Anglican Church is the largest Protestant denomination followed by Presbyterian and Seventh-day Adventist churches.

Most churches have denomination-based schools. But the schools are open to all students.

There is a small Muslim population descended mostly from Gujarati Indian immigrants who went to Grenada during the colonial period and set up merchant shops.

Culture

The culture of Grenada is a product of Africa and Europe.

On the European side, it was the French who first brought their culture to the island since they were the first external power to occupy the island.

The British also have had profound influence on Grenada even more so than the French. They ruled the island longer than the French did.

The influence of African slaves and their descendants is also clearly evident on the island. It has endured even more because the vast majority of the people are of African origin, descended from slaves. Their ties to Africa are reflected in many ways including attire and hairstyles; the kind of music they compose and the way they dance; the way they cook and the kind of foods they cook; the stories they tell which can be traced all the way back to Africa and much more.

The slave trade and its abolition also had an impact on

India.

After the slave trade and slavery were abolished, the British colonial rulers in Grenada and elsewhere in the Caribbean recruited workers from India. They were indentured servants and a very large number of them were taken to those islands.

Many of them remained in the Caribbean. For example, among the more than 3,000 East Indian indentured servants who ended up in Grenada by 1885, only about 400 returned to India. Those who stayed became an integral part of Grenadian society.

The Indians later on assimilated with the existing Africans, Europeans and members of other ethnic groups, intermarrying with each other. This inter-racial mixing has influenced the culture and cuisine of Grenada in a significant way.

In 1957, Grenadians of Indian descent celebrated the 100th anniversary of their first arrival on the island. And even today, Indian Arrival Day celebration is an important event in the Indo-Grenadian community.

French influence also has had an impact on Grenada. But the influence is less visible in this island nation than it is on some of the other Caribbean islands, especially those which were ones ruled by France.

The most visible symbol of French influence on Grenada is etched in surnames and place names. French influence is also evident in the language, especially Grenadian Creole. Everyday language is laced with French words and the local dialect or Patois.

Stronger French influence is found in the well-seasoned spicy food and styles of cooking similar to those found in New Orleans in the southern American state of Louisiana. And some French architecture has survived on the island of Grenada from the 1700s.

The island's culture is also heavily influenced by the African roots of most of the Grenadians. But Indian and Carib Amerindian influence is also clearly evident – in foods, for example, in terms of East Indian culture - dhal puri, rotis, Indian sweets, cassava and curries in the cuisine.

The islanders' African and Carib Amerindian heritage plays an influential role in many aspects of Grenada's culture.

As with other islands in the Caribbean, cricket is the national and most popular sport and is an intrinsic part of Grenadian culture.

An important aspect of Grenadian culture is the tradition of story telling, with folk tales bearing both African and French influences.

The character, Anansi, a spider god who is a trickster, originated in West Africa and is prevalent on other Caribbean islands.

Also, French influence can be seen in *La Diablesse*, a well-dressed she-devil, and *Ligaroo* (from Loup Garoux), a werewolf.

Cuisine

Special dishes reflect the cultural diversity of Grenada. The "oildown" is considered to be the national dish. The phrase "oil-down" refers to a dish cooked in coconut milk until all the milk is absorbed, leaving a bit of coconut oil at the bottom of the pot.

Oildown or Oil Down – the national dish – is a combination of breadfruit, coconut milk, turmeric (misnamed saffron), dumplings, callaloo (taro leaves) and a salted meat such as saltfish accra (codfish), smoked herring or salt beef.

It's often cooked in a large pot commonly referred to by locals as a karhee, or curry pot.

Early recipes since the days of slavery – still prevalent today – involve a mixture of salted pigtail, pigs feet (trotters), salt beef and chicken, and dumplings made from flour, as well as breadfruit, green banana, yam and potatoes. Callaloo leaves are sometimes used to retain steam and for extra flavour.

The dish is common at family and other gatherings at the beach.

There is some debate in the Caribbean – or West Indies – about the origin of the dish, with some experts attributing it to other islands like Barbados or Trinidad & Tobago. But there is no question it has African cultural elements in terms of preparation.

Popular street foods in Grenada include aloo pie, doubles and dal puri served wrapped around a curry, commonly goat, and bakes and fish cakes.

Sweets include kurma, guava cheese, fudge or barfi, tamarind balls, rum and raisin ice cream and currant rolls.

Music of Grenada

Foods aren't the only important aspect of Grenadian culture. Music, dance, and festivals are also extremely important.

Soca, calypso, and reggae set the mood for Grenada's annual carnival activities.

Also, rap music has became famous among Grenadian youths and there have been numerous young rappers emerging from the island's underground rap scene.

Zouk is also being slowly introduced into the island.

The music of Grenada includes the work of several major musicians such as Eddie Bullen, David Emmanuel who is one of the best-selling reggae performers, and the internationally renowned Mighty Sparrow, a calypsonian who was born in Grenada but who later became a Trinidadian.

The island of Grenada is also known for jazz including one of its most well-known performers, Kingsley Etienne, a keyboardist; while the Grenadian-American Joe Country

& the Islanders have made a name in country music.

African dances brought to Grenada survive in an evolved form, as have European quadrilles and picquets.

Some of the most popular recent dances include Heel-and-Toe and Carriacou Big Drum, with popular dancers such as Willie Readhead, Thelma Phillips, Renalph Gebon, and and the Beewee Ballet.

Independence in 1974 launched a Grenadian national identity which was exemplified in the calypso of the time which tended to be intensely patriotic.

More modern calypso performers have experimented in various forms using political commentary and poetry to expand the possibilities of Grenadian calypso. Indian influences have also changed the sound of Grenadian calypso.

Carriacou

Many years of domination by the British and the French have left behind influences on the island of Carriacou in musical forms such as lullabies and reels, cantique, chanteys and quadrilles.

Located north of Grenada, Carriacou island is best-known for the Big drum Afro-Caribbean song-style. Big Drum dates back to at least the late 1700s.

Carriacou's Afro-Caribbean population is divided into "nations," each of which has a distinct rhythm that identifies it. Big Drum glorifies the ancestors of these nations which include the Manding, Temne, Igbo, Kongo, Cromanti and others.

The Cromanti, being the biggest "nation," begins the Big Drum ceremony with a song called "Cromanti Cudjo" (or *"Beg Pardon"*); this is followed by the other nations' songs, all of which are based on short, declamatory phrases with choruses, accompanied by two *boula* drums and a single, higher-pitched *cut drum*, both of which are made from rum barrels.

Big Drum music is used to honour the memory of the dead if the family of the deceased is not able to have the traditional Tombstone Feast.

The funeral music of Carriacou is a major part of the island's folk music.

Carriacouan religion centres on reverence for the "Old Parents," the apocryphal founders of the island's society.

The saraca funeral rite practised on Carriacou and throughout the Grenadines involves music, story telling and feasting. Saraca songs include both European and African lyrics. African elements, such as the call-and-response style, are often present.

Music and Festivals

Music plays a prominent role in Grenadian culture best demonstrated by carnivals which include competitions. For example, there are soca and calypso competitions held in August every year.

The music of soca, calypso, and reggae is also used on minibuses whose owners compete for the loudest and sometimes fastest bus service.

Zouk music, another important feature of Grenada's musical scene, has been imported recently from Francophone islands in the Caribbean. It may eventually become an integral part of Grenadian culture if it continues to grow on the island, with performers of this musical form giving it a unique identity which is typical Grenadian in terms of expression, lyrical content, performance and style.

Besides Independence Day, other major national events in Grenada include the National Dance Festival.

Chapter Nine:
Jamaica

JAMAICA is an island nation of the Greater Antilles in the Caribbean Sea. It's about 90 miles south of Cuba and 120 miles west of Hispaniola which is an island comprising Haiti and the Dominican Republic. It has an area of 4,300 square miles.

Its indigenous Arawakan-speaking Taino inhabitants named the island *Xaymaca*, meaning the "Land of Wood and Water," or the "Land of Springs."

It once was a Spanish possession known as *Santiago*. In 1655, it became an English and later a British colony known as "Jamaica." It won independence in 1962.

With 2.8 million people, it's the third most populous Anglophone country in the Americas after the United States and Canada.

It's also the fourth most populous country in the Caribbean after Cuba, the Dominican Republic, and Haiti in that descending order; while Trinidad and Tobago is the fifth most populous nation in the Caribbean.

In terms of area, Jamaica is the third-largest island in the Caribbean after Cuba and Hispaniola. Cuba is the largest and most populous of all the islands – and island nations – in the Caribbean.

Kingston is the largest city in Jamaica and the country's capital.

History

When Christopher Columbus arrived in what is now Jamaica, he claimed the island for Spain. But the island it was not really colonised until after his death.

Those were also the days when pirates reigned supreme on the high seas and Spain held the island against many buccaneer raids at what was then the main city which is now called Spanish Town.

Eventually England claimed the island in a raid but the Spanish settlers and their home country of Spain did not relinquish their claim to the island until 1670.

Jamaica became a base of operations for buccaneers; one of the most famous was Captain Henry Morgan. In return, the buccaneers – on behalf of England – kept the other colonial powers from attacking the island.

The island also became one of the most prominent destinations for Africans sold into slavery. Most of the African slaves came from West Africa and they became the most important labour force for the island's economy when they worked on plantations on the island.

The plantations were mostly for the production of sugar and sugarcane became the most important export for the island.

Many slaves arrived in Jamaica during the same time other enslaved Africans arrived in the United States. In fact, the Caribbean islands, including Jamaica, also served as a transit point for slaves destined for the United States.

There were a lot of racial tensions during that period because of the injustices African slaves suffered at the hands of their masters. The injustices led to conflict and Jamaica had one of the highest instances of slave uprisings in the Caribbean.

British rule

When the British seized Jamaica in 1655, Spanish resistance continued for some years, in some cases with the help of the maroons, but Spain never succeeded in retaking the island.

Under early English rule, Jamaica became a haven for privateers, buccaneers, and occasionally outright pirates: Christopher Myngs, Edward Mansvelt, and most famously, Henry Morgan.

In one of his songs, "You Can't Blame the Youth," Peter Tosh sings about Henry Morgan and other notorious historical figures who have been wrongly glorified, saying:

> You teach the youths about Christopher Columbus
> And you said he was a very great man
> You teach the youth about Marco Polo
> And you said he was a very great man
>
> You teach the youths about the pirate Hawkins
> And you said he was a very great man
> You teach the youths about the pirate Morgan
> And you said he was a very great man
>
> All these so-called great men were doing
> robbing, raping, kidnapping and killing

Besides sugar, another major crop grown by the English settlers in Jamaica was coffee. And like sugarcane, the cultivation of coffee was also entirely dependent on the labour extracted from African slaves.

For more than 150 years, the cultivation of sugarcane and coffee by African slaves made Jamaica one of the most valuable colonial possessions in the world.

The colony's slaves, who outnumbered their white masters by a ratio of 20 to 1 in 1800, mounted over a dozen major slave conspiracies and uprisings during the 1700s including the famous Tacky's Revolt in 1760.

Escaped slaves known as Maroons established independent communities in the mountainous interior which the British were unable to suppress despite major attempts in the 1730s and 1790s to do so.

One Maroon community was expelled from the island after the Second Maroon War in the 1790s. The Maroons who were expelled after that war eventually became part of the core of the Creole community of Sierra Leone.

Also, the British colonial government enlisted the Maroons in capturing escaped plantation slaves. The British also used Jamaica's free people of colour, 10,000 strong by 1800, to keep the enslaved population in check.

During the Christmas holiday of 1831, a large-scale slave revolt known as the Baptist War erupted. It was originally organised as a peaceful strike by Samuel Sharpe. But the rebellion was not successful. It was suppressed by the militia of the Jamaican plantocracy and by the British garrison ten days later in early 1832.

Although the rebellion was suppressed, it caused some damage, loss of life and property, prompting the British parliament to hold two enquiries. The results of these inquiries contributed greatly to the abolition of slavery as of 1 August 1834 throughout the British empire.

However, the Jamaican slaves remained bound to their former owners' service, albeit with a guarantee of rights, until 1838 under what was called the Apprenticeship System.

The freed population still faced significant hardships, marked by the October 1865 Morant Bay rebellion led by and Paul Bogle. It was brutally repressed.

George William Gordon, a friend of Paul Bogle, was hanged because he was thought to have contributed to the riot even though he was not a part of its organisation or execution.

There was also a major change in the island's economy which had depended almost exclusively on sugar for so long. The sugar crop was declining in importance in the late 19th century and the colony diversified into the production of bananas.

In 1872, the capital of Jamaica was moved from Spanish Town to Kingston, a port city; the port city had far outstripped the inland Spanish Town in size and sophistication and was considered the right place to be the island's capital.

In 1866, the Jamaican legislature renounced its powers and the country became a crown colony. But some measure of self-government was restored in the 1880s when islanders gained the right to elect nine members of the island's legislative council.

The establishment of crown colony rule resulted – during the next few decades – in the growth of a middle class of low-level public officials and police officers drawn from the mass of the population whose social and political advancement was blocked by the colonial authorities.

Then came the Great Depression in the 1930s. The depression had a serious impact on the fledgling middle class and on the working class in Jamaica during that period.

The economic hardship led to other problems. In the spring of 1938, sugar and dock workers revolted on the island. Although the revolt was suppressed, it led to significant changes including the emergence of an organised labour movement and a competitive party system.

Independent Jamaica

Jamaica gained a degree of local political control in the mid-1940's.

The first political party to be established was the People's National Party (PNP) founded in 1938. Its main rival, the Jamaican Labour Party (JLP) was established five years later.

The first elections under universal adult suffrage were held in 1944.

Jamaica and nine other British colonies in the Caribbean formed the Federation of the West Indies in 1958. But Jamaica withdrew after its voters rejected in 1961 their country's membership in the federation.

Not long thereafter, Jamaica won independence from the United Kingdom on 6 August 1962 and remained a member of the Commonwealth of Nations. The island's first prime minister was Alexander Bustamante of the Jamaica Labour Party (JLP).

Initially, power swapped between the People's National Party and the Jamaican Labour Party.

Michael Manley was the first PNP prime minister in 1972. He introduced socialist policies and relations with Cuba. His second-term elections marked the start of repeated political violence.

When the PNP lost power in 1980, Edward Seaga immediately began to reverse the policies of his predecessor, bringing in privatisation and seeking closer ties with the United States.

When the PNP and Manley returned to power in 1989, they continued the more moderate policies and were returned in the elections of 1993 and 1998. Manley resigned for health reasons in 1992 and was succeeded as leader of the PNP by Percival Patterson.

The island of Jamaica has also been a source of

immigrants to other countries for a long time.

In the late 1800s and early 1900s, many Jamaicans migrated to Central America, Cuba and the Dominican Republic to work in the banana and canefields.

In the 1950s, the primary destination was the United Kingdom. But the British parliament passed a restrictive immigration law in 1962 which drastically reduced the number of immigrants from its former colonies and elsewhere entering the country.

After the restriction was imposed, Jamaicans emigrating from their homeland turned their attention to the United States as their primary destination, followed by Canada.

The heaviest flow of emigration particularly to New York and Miami occurred during the 1990s and continues today because of worsening economic conditions on the island.

New York, Miami and Fort Lauderdale in Florida are among the U.S. cities with the largest Jamaican population. In New York City alone, more than half of Jamaican immigrants live in Brooklyn. Remittances from Jamaican communities in the United States, the United Kingdom, and Canada make increasingly significant contributions to Jamaica's economy.

A Closer look since colonial times

In 1660, the population of Jamaica was about 4,500 whites and some 1,500 blacks. As early as the 1670s, blacks formed a majority of the population.

When the English captured Jamaica in 1655, the Spanish colonists fled leaving a large number of African slaves. Rather than be re-enslaved by the English, they escaped into the hilly, mountainous regions of the island, joining those who had previously escaped from the Spanish to live with the Tainos.

These runaway slaves, who came to be known as the Jamaican Maroons, fought the British during the 18th century. The name is still used today for their modern descendants.

During the long years of slavery, Maroons established free communities in the mountainous interior of Jamaica, maintaining their freedom and independence for generations.

And during its first 200 years of British rule, Jamaica became one of the world's leading sugar-exporting, slave-dependent nations, producing more than 77,000 tons of sugar annually between 1820 and 1824.

After the abolition of the slave trade – but not slavery itself – in 1807, the British imported Indian and Chinese workers as indentured servants to supplement the labour pool. Descendants of indentured servants of Asian and Chinese origin continue to live in Jamaica today and they constitute an integral part of Jamaican society.

By the beginning of the 19th century, Jamaica's heavy reliance on slavery resulted in blacks – Africans – outnumbering whites – Europeans – by a ratio of almost 20 to 1.

Even though England had outlawed the importation of slaves, some were still smuggled into the colonies in the Caribbean. Slaves ships continued to sail from Africa to the Americas even as late as the 1840s as the case of *The Amistad* demonstrates involving slaves of the Mende tribe captured in Sierra Leone.

Some slave traders also evaded anti-slavery patrols on the West African coast by turning their attention to what is now Tanzania and Mozambique, although the number of slaves taken from East Africa to the Americas was much smaller than the number of those who taken from the western parts of the continent.

The British government drew-up laws regimenting the abolition of slavery. But they also included instructions for the improvement of the slaves' way of life. These instructions included a ban on the use of whips in the field; a ban on the flogging of women; notification that slaves were to be allowed religious instruction; a requirement that slaves be given an extra free day during the week when they could sell their products; and a ban of Sunday markets.

The measures applied to all the British colonies where slavery had been practised by the colonial power. However, in Jamaica, these measures were resisted by the House of Assembly. The Assembly claimed that the slaves were content and objected to interference by the British parliament in the island's affairs, although many slave owners feared possible revolts.

Following a series of rebellions, and changing attitudes in Great Britain, the British parliament formally abolished slavery in 1834, with full emancipation from chattel slavery declared in 1838.

In 1834, the population of Jamaica was 371,070 of whom 15,000 were whites, 5,000 free blacks, 40,000 'coloureds' or people of mixed race, and 311,070 slaves.

There were other changes on the island of Jamaica introduced by the colonial rulers. In the 1800s, the British established a number of botanical gardens. These included the Castleton Garden set up in 1862 to replace the Bath Garden (created in 1779) which was subject to flooding. Bath Garden was the site for planting breadfruit brought to Jamaica from the Pacific by Captain William Bligh. Other gardens were the Cinchona Plantation founded in 1868 and the Hope Garden founded in 1874.

In 1872, Kingston became the island's capital and, in the years that followed, many changes took place across the spectrum.

In 1945, Sir Horace Hector Hearne became Jamaica's Chief Justice and Keeper of the Records. He headed the Supreme Court in Kingston between 1945 and 1950/1951. He then moved to Kenya where he was appointed Chief Justice.

Jamaica slowly gained increasing independence from the United Kingdom and in 1958, it became a province in the Federation of the West Indies. It was a federation of British colonies in the region which were then collectively known as the British West Indies. Jamaica attained full independence by leaving the federation in 1962.

The end of colonial rule was the dawn of a new era.

Strong economic growth averaging approximately 6 per cent per annum marked the first ten years of independence under conservative governments which were led successively by Prime Ministers Alexander Bustamante, Donald Sangster and Hugh Shearer.

The growth was fuelled by strong investments in the mining sector dominated by bauxite for the production of aluminium as well as in tourism and in the manufacturing industry and, to a lesser extent, in the agricultural sector.

However, the optimism of the first decade was accompanied by a growing sense of inequality, and a sense that the benefits of growth were not being shared by the urban poor, let alone those in the rural areas. This, combined with the effects of a slowdown in the global economy in 1970, prompted the electorate to change government, electing the PNP (People's National Party) in 1972.

And despite efforts to implement more socially equitable policies in the areas of health and education, Jamaica continued to lag economically, with its gross national product having fallen in 1980 to some 25% below the 1972 level.

Rising foreign and local debt, accompanied by large fiscal deficits, resulted in the invitation of the International Monetary Fund (IMF) financing from the United States and Western donors, and the imposition of IMF austerity measures with an interest rate per year higher than 25%; the same kind of structural adjustment programmes (SAPs) which caused untold hardship and suffering on hundreds of millions of people in Africa – and in other parts of the Third World – in the 1980s and 1990s and beyond.

Economic deterioration continued into the mid-1980s, exacerbated by a number of factors; the first and third largest alumina producers – Alpart and Alcoa – closed, and there was a significant reduction in production by the second largest producer, Alcan.

In addition, tourism decreased and Reynolds Jamaica Mines, Ltd. left the Jamaican industry.

Government and politics

Jamaica is a parliamentary democracy under a multi-party system patterned after the British model.

The government is headed by the prime minister who exercises executive functions and runs the country with his cabinet.

Queen Elizabeth II is the head of state. She officially uses the title "Queen of Jamaica" when she visits the country or performs duties overseas on Jamaica's behalf.

Her representative in Jamaica is the governor-general. The governor-general is nominated by the prime minister and by the cabinet but is formally appointed to his post by the British monarch – Queen Elizabeth II – in her official capacity as Jamaica's head of state.

All the members of the cabinet are appointed by the governor-general on the advice of the prime minister. It's the prime minister who chooses his cabinet. The governor-general plays only a ceremonial role of appointing cabinet members.

The monarch and the governor-general serve largely ceremonial roles, apart from having potent reserve power to dismiss the prime minister or parliament.

Geography

One of Jamaica's most prominent physical features is Blue mountains located inland. The island is surrounded by a narrow coastal plain.

Most major towns and cities are located on the coast. Major towns and cities include the capital Kingston, Portmore, Spanish Town, Mandeville, Ocho Rios, Port Antonio, Negril, and Montego Bay.

The Kingston Harbour is one of the largest natural harbours in the world.

There are several tourist attractions scattered across the country. They include Dunn's River Falls in St. Ann, YS Falls in St. Elizabeth, the Blue Lagoon in Portland, and Port Royal which was the site of an earthquake that helped form the island's Palisadoes.

The climate in Jamaica is tropical, with hot and humid weather, although higher inland regions are more temperate. Some regions on the south coast, such as the Liguanea Plain and the Pedro Plains, are relatively dry rain-shadow areas.

Jamaica lies in the hurricane belt of the Atlantic Ocean; as a result, the island sometimes experiences significant storm damage.

Hurricanes Charlie and Gilbert hit Jamaica directly in 1951 and 1988, respectively, causing major damage and many deaths.

In the 2000s, hurricanes Ivan, Dean, and Gustav also brought severe weather to the island.

At its greatest extent, Jamaica is 146 miles long and it varies between 21 and 52miles in width.

With an area of 4,213 square miles, Jamaica is the largest island of the Commonwealth Caribbean – comprising former British colonies once collectively known as the British West Indies – and the third largest of the Greater Antilles after Cuba and Hispaniola.

A number of small islands are located along the southern coast of Jamaica. They include the Port Royal Cays; Pedro Bank, an area of shallow seas with a number of cays which are low islands or reefs; and Morant Bank with the Morant Cays in the southeast. Morant Point is the easternmost point of mainland Jamaica.

Coasts

The coastline of Jamaica is one of many contrasts. The northeast shore is severely eroded by the ocean. There are many small inlets in the rugged coastline, but no coastal plain of any extent. A narrow strip of plains along the northern coast offers calm seas and white sand beaches. Behind the beaches is a flat raised plain of uplifted coral reef.

The southern coast has small stretches of plains lined by black sand beaches. These are backed by cliffs of limestone where the plateaus end. In many stretches with no coastal plain, the cliffs drop 984 feet straight to the sea. In the southwest, broad plains stretch inland for a number of miles.

The Black River flows 43 miles through the largest of these plains. The swamplands of the Great Morass and the Upper Morass fill much of the plains. The western coastline contains the island's finest beaches.

Climate

Two types of climate are found in Jamaica. An upland tropical climate prevails on the windward side of the mountains, whereas a semiarid climate predominates on the leeward side.

Warm trade winds from the east and northeast bring rainfall throughout the year. The rainfall is heaviest from

May to October, with peaks in those two months.

Rainfall is much greater in the mountain areas facing the north and east. Where the higher elevations of the John Crow Mountains and the Blue Mountains catch the rain from the moisture-laden winds, rainfall exceeds 200 inches per year.

Since the southwestern half of the island lies in the rain shadow of the mountains, it has a semiarid climate and receives fewer than 29.9 inches of rainfall annually.

Temperatures are fairly constant throughout the year, averaging 77 to 86°F in the lowlands and 59 to 71.6°F at higher elevations. Temperatures may dip to below 50°F at the peaks of the Blue Mountains.

In addition to the northeast trade winds, the island receives refreshing onshore breezes during the day and cooling offshore breezes at night. These are known in Jamaica as the "Doctor Breeze" and the "Undertaker's Breeze," respectively.

In addition to major hurricanes which have hit the island, several other powerful hurricanes have passed near the island with damaging effects. In 1980, for example, Hurricane Allen destroyed nearly all of Jamaica's banana crop.

In recent years, Hurricane Ivan swept past the island causing heavy damage and a number of deaths in 2004. In 2005, Hurricanes Dennis and Emily brought heavy rains to the island. And Hurricane Dean caused some deaths and heavy damage to Jamaica in August 2007.

The first recorded hurricane to hit Jamaica was in 1519.

The island has been struck by tropical cyclones regularly. During two of the coldest periods in the last 250 years – 1780s to the 1810 – the frequency of hurricanes in the Jamaica region was unusually high. Another peak of activity occurred in the 1910s, the coldest decade of the 20th century.

On the other hand, hurricane formation was greatly

diminished from 1968 to 1994, which for some reason coincides with the great Sahel drought.

Jamiaca was also hit by a severe storm on 29 September 2010 which killed some people and caused extensive damage. According to a report by David McFadden of the Associated Press (AP) from Kingston, Jamaica, on Wednesday evening (Eastern Standard Time – EST – in the United States), 29 September 2010, "2 Known Dead, 12 Missing After Storm Soaks Jamaica":

"Tropical Storm Nicole caused flooding and mudslides across Jamaica on Wednesday, leaving two confirmed dead and at least 12 more missing, even as the drenching system moved north and dissipated over the Florida straits.

The outer bands of the storm hammered Jamaica, toppling bridges and knocking out power to thousands. Many streets were filled with gushing brown torrents of water, prompting Prime Minister Bruce Golding to urge people to stay indoors.

Floodwaters battered squatter communities perched uneasily on the slopes of gullies that crisscross the sprawling capital of Kingston. One slide killed a 14-year-old boy, known to his neighbors as Buju, who was found in an eddy of muddy water. The rest of his family — including four sisters, the youngest just 3-years-old — had not been found by Wednesday evening.

'He was a fun boy. He loved to sing, he loved to play football. It's not right, the whole family lost,' said Munchie Fuller, a 23-year-old neighbor who watched terrified as a chunk of her own concrete house in Sandy Gully was swept into the raging waters before dawn.

Another resident, Lyndon Bennett, said the people in the shantytown who live along the gully are warned repeatedly to move for their own safety but most refuse to relocate.

'There's not a proper foundation there, the gully is just stone and dirt. People are told not to live there, but when you've got no other options you've just got to make ends meet. It's a real tragedy,' Bennett said.

The storm, which had sustained winds of 40 mph (65 kph) earlier in the day, broke apart over the Atlantic, though the U.S. National Hurricane Center in Miami warned that there were still large areas of heavy rain.

Jamaican Information Minister Daryl Vaz said two people were confirmed dead but warned that the toll could be higher from the flash floods and mudslides. He said 12 people were missing.

Emergency shelters were opened for thousands of Jamaicans who live in ramshackle homes along gullies. Major hospitals were treating only emergency cases. Officials said about 30 percent of the power utility's customers were without power. Some bridges collapsed in the rushing water.

'All in all, there has been a lot of damage done to infrastructure,' Vaz said. 'It's a serious blow to the country.'

In a rural area of St. Elizabeth parish, people told government officials that two farmers in the town of Flagaman were washed away by murky floodwaters and presumed dead. Another man was reportedly swept away while trying to cross rushing Hope River in Kingston.

Floods flattened fields of bananas, scallions and sweet pepper as the storm's outer edges raked the island.

The storm also soaked Cuba but no deaths were reported.

In Cuba, state-controlled television showed images of rain flooding roads and highways, especially around the eastern city of Santiago, but there were no reports of major damage. Far to the west in Havana, it wasn't even raining and there was no flooding."

Another report, on the same day, on the same storm had a higher number of deaths. According to Kevin Gray of Reuters news agency in his report from Miami, Florida, "Tropical Storm Nicole Kills Eight in Jamaica":

"Short-lived Tropical Storm Nicole triggered flash flooding that killed eight people in Jamaica and dumped heavy rain on Florida, Cuba, the Cayman Islands and the Bahamas on Wednesday.

The broad and ragged storm formed on Wednesday morning and dissipated Wednesday afternoon, and U.S. and Cuban meteorologists disagreed on whether it ever actually was a tropical storm at all.

Forecasters at the U.S. National Hurricane Center in Miami pegged its peak sustained winds at 40 miles per hour, just over the 39 mph threshold to become a named storm.

Cuban forecasters put the top winds at 37 mph and disagreed that it was a tropical storm when it crossed the island.

'No tropical storm exists,' Cuba's top meteorologist, Jorge Rubiera, said on national television.

U.S. forecasters said Nicole had a poorly defined center of circulation and had been 'a marginal system.'

'Their interpretation is that they don't think it's a storm ... They're on one side of the margin and we're on the other,' Richard Pasch, a senior hurricane specialist in Miami, said before the storm was downgraded.

Nicole degenerated into a broad mass of thunderstorms that were forecast to move north-northeast over the Atlantic between Florida and the Bahamas on Wednesday night and then over the U.S. mid-Atlantic states by Friday.

All tropical storm warnings were dropped but the system was still dumping heavy rain on Jamaica, the Cayman Islands, Cuba, the Bahamas and southern Florida.

There was still a threat of flash flooding and mudslides in mountainous areas, the Hurricane Center forecasters said.

In Jamaica, the storm triggered floods that drowned two elderly men and a family of six.

A man in his seventies drowned in the village of Unity,

north of Kingston, and a man in his 60s drowned in the southwest Jamaican town of Flagaman. Both were trying to walk home from village pubs when they were swept off by rising waters.

Police said a house occupied by a family of seven collapsed near the U.S. Embassy in the Liguanea area northeast of Kingston. A boy was rescued after citizens rushed to his aid but six members of his family were carried off by floodwaters and were confirmed to have drowned.

In Cuba, the heaviest rains fell in the central part of the island, where they were a welcome relief from a prolonged drought that had drained reservoirs and caused water shortages. Nearly eight inches of rain fell in the central province of Sancti Spiritus.

'These rains are a gift from heaven. I hope they go on for two or three days,' said Mariela Diaz, an officer worker in the city of Sancti Spiritus.

(Writing by Jane Sutton; additional reporting by Jeff Franks in Havana and Horace George in Kingston; editing by Eric Walsh)."

Vegetation

Although most of Jamaica's native vegetation has been stripped in order to make room for cultivation, some areas have been left virtually undisturbed since the time of Columbus.

Indigenous vegetation can be found along the northern coast from Rio Bueno to Discovery Bay, in the highest parts of the Blue Mountains, and in the heart of the Cockpit Country.

Demographics

Ethnic origins

Jamaica's population mainly consists of people of African descent. There is also a large population of multiracial Jamaicans.

The largest minority groups are Jamaicans of Indian and Chinese ancestry. There are at least 160,000 of them, according to the 2001 census in a total population of more than 2.5 million.

Lebanese, Syrian, English, Scottish, Irish and German Jamaicans are small minorities. There are about 3,000-4,000 of them altogether.

But in recent years, immigration has increased. Many immigrants who have entered Jamaica have come mainly from China, Haiti, Cuba, Colombia, and other Latin American countries; 20,000 Latin Americans currently live in Jamaica. And about 7,000 Americans also live in Jamaica.

This topic is somewhat contentious with several respected sources giving different figures. In alphabetical order these are:

CIA Fact Book: black 91.2%, mixed 6.2%, other or unknown 2.6% (2001 census).

University of the West Indies: 76.3% African descent, 15.1% Afro-European, 3.4% East Indian and Afro-East Indian, 3.2% Caucasian, 1.2% Chinese and 0.8% Other.

Language

The official language of Jamaica is English. But the vast majority of Jamaicans – or Jamaicans in general – primarily speak an English-African Creole language known as Jamaican Patois which has become known widely through the spread of reggae music.

Jamaican English

Jamaican English or Jamaican Standard English is a dialect of English spoken in Jamaica. It melds parts of both American English and British English dialects. Typically, it uses British English spellings and often rejects American English spellings.

Although the distinction between the two is best described as a continuum rather than a solid line, it's not to be confused with Jamaican Patois – what linguists call Jamaican Creole – nor with the vocabulary and language usage of the Rastafari movement.

"Patois" or Patwa is a French term referring to regional languages of France which include some Creole languages. But in Jamaica, the term refers to Jamaican Creole which Jamaicans have traditionally seen as "broken" or incorrect Standard English.

Yet it has its own legitimacy as a functional language of a particular people with their own identity and has won wide acceptance among its users the same way Black English – or Ebonics – has among millions of African Americans.

In that sense, it's considered to be a language, not just gibberish, which reflects the identity of a group of people and their history in a particular historical context.

But it's definitely not Standard English anymore than Ebonics is.

Some people dismiss it as – ignorance; a judgement that applies to Black English or Ebonics as well.

Grammar

Jamaican Standard English is grammatically similar to British Standard English. Recently, however, due to

Jamaica's proximity to the United States and the resulting close economic ties and high rates of migration – as well as the ubiquity of American cultural/entertainment products such as movies, cable television and popular music – the influence of American English has been increasing steadily. As a result, constructions or sentence structures such as "I don't have" or "you don't need" are almost universally preferred over "I haven't got" or "you needn't."

Vocabulary

The Irish accent is a major influence on the accent of Jamaican English today.

Recent American influence is also obvious in the lexicon. For example, babies sleep in "cribs" and wear "diapers" [or "pampers"]. Some people live in "apartments" – not in "flats" as the British say. Some people also live in "townhouses" – American English again.

Generally, older vocabulary tends to be British: babies wear "nappies," not "diapers." Cars have "bonnets" and not "hoods" which is an American term; they also have "windscreens" – Americans say cars have "windshields."

Children study "maths" – Americans say "math" without an "s." Children also use "rubbers" to erase their mistakes and wish they were on "holiday." Americans say children use "erasers" – not "rubbers" – to erase their mistakes; and they wish they were on "vacation," not on "holiday."

The vocabulary in Jamaica is influenced by newer phenomena introduced into the country. Such phenomena are typically "imported" together with their American names.

An interesting use of mixed British and American vocabulary is with automobiles where the American term "trunk" is almost universally used in Jamaica instead of the British term "boot."

The British term "sleeping policeman" is used instead of the American term "Speed Bump," while the engine covering is always referred to by the British term "bonnet." This is probably because the American term, "hood," is used in Jamaica as a vulgar slang for penis.

Naturally, Jamaican Standard English also uses many local words borrowed from Jamaican Patois: "duppy" for "ghost"; "higgler" for "informal vendor"; and some terms for local foods, such as "ackee," "callaloo," "guinep," and "bammy."

Pronunciation

Jamaican Standard pronunciation differs greatly from Jamaican Patois pronunciation. But it's clearly and recognizably Caribbean.

Giveaway features include the characteristic pronunciation of the diphthong in words like "cow" which is more closed and rounded than in Received Pronunciation (RP) or General American (GenAm); the pronunciation of the *strut* vowel (again, more closed than the RP or GenAm version, though not as closed as in the Creole); semi-rhoticity, i.e. the dropping of the "-r" in words like "water" (at the end of unstressed syllables) and "market" (before a consonant); but not in words like "car" or "dare" (stressed syllables at the end of the word).

Merger of the diphthongs in "fair" and "fear" takes place both in Jamaican Standard and Jamaican Patois, resulting in those two words (and many others, like "bear" and "beer") becoming homophones. (Standard speakers typically pronounce both closer to "air," while Creole speakers render them as "ear"). The short "a" sound (man, hat) is very open, similar to its Irish versions.

Language use: Standard versus Patois

Jamaican Standard and Jamaican Patois exist together in a post-creole speech continuum.

Creole is used by most people for everyday, informal situations – it's the language most Jamaicans use at home and are most familiar with; it's also the language of most local popular music.

Jamaican Standard, on the other hand, is the language of education, high culture, government, the media and official/formal communications. It's also the native language of a small minority of Jamaicans (typically upper class and upper/traditional middle class).

Most Creole-dominant speakers have a fair command of Standard English, through schooling and exposure to official culture and mass media; their receptive skills (understanding of Standard English) are typically much better than their productive skills (their own intended Standard English statements often show signs of Creole interference).

Most writing in Jamaica is done in Standard English (including private notes and correspondence).

Jamaican Patois has no standardized spelling, and has only recently been taught in some schools. As a result, the majority of Jamaicans can read and write Standard English only, and have trouble deciphering written dialect (in which the writer tries to reflect characteristic structures and pronunciations to differing degrees, without compromising readability).

Written Patois appears mostly in literature, especially in folkloristic "dialect poems"; in humouristic newspaper columns; and most recently, on Internet chat sites frequented by younger Jamaicans who seem to have a more positive attitude toward their own language use than their parents.

While, for the sake of simplicity, it's customary to

describe Jamaican speech in terms of Standard versus Creole, a clear-cut dichotomy does not adequately describe the actual language use of most Jamaicans. Between the two extremes – "broad Patois" on one end of the spectrum, and "perfect" Standard on the other – there are various in-between varieties.

This situation typically results when a Creole language is in constant contact with its standard (superstrate or lexifier language) and is called a creole speech continuum.

The least prestigious (most Creole) variety is called the basilect; the Standard (or high prestige) variety the acrolect; and in-between versions are known as mesolects.

Consider, for example, the following forms:

"im ah wok oba deh suh" (basilect).
"im workin ova deh suh" (low mesolect).
"(H)e (h)is workin' over dere" (high mesolect).
"He is working over there." (acrolect).

(As noted above, the "r" in "over" is not pronounced in any variety, but the one in "dere" or "there" is.)

Jamaicans choose from the varieties available to them according to the situation.

A Creole-dominant speaker will choose a higher variety for formal occasions like official business or a wedding speech, and a lower one for relating to friends; a Standard-dominant speaker is likely to employ a lower variety when shopping at the market than at her workplace.

Code-switching can also be metaphoric (e.g., a Standard-dominant speaker switching to a lower variety for humoristic purposes, or to express solidarity).

Jamaican Patois

Jamaican Patois, known locally as Patois (Patwa) or

Jamaican, and called Jamaican Creole by linguists, is an English-lexified creole language with West African influences spoken primarily in Jamaica and the Jamaican diaspora. It's not to be confused with Jamaican English nor with the Rastafarian use of English.

The language developed in the 17th century when slaves from West and Central Africa were exposed to, learned and nativised the vernacular and dialectical forms of English spoken by their masters: British English and Hiberno English.

Jamaican Patois features a creole continuum (a *linguistic continuum*) – meaning that the variety of the language closest to the lexifier language (the acrolect) can not be distinguished systematically from intermediate varieties (collectively referred to as the mesolect) nor even from the most divergent rural varieties (collectively referred to as the basilect). Jamaicans themselves usually refer to their dialect as patois, a French term without a precise linguistic definition.

Significant Jamaican-speaking communities exist among Jamaicans who live in Miami, New York City, Toronto, Hartford in the American state of Connecticut, Washington, D.C., London in the UK, and in the Central American countries of Nicaragua, Costa Rica, and Panama on the Caribbean coast.

A mutually intelligible variety is found in San Andres y Providencia Islands, Colombia, brought to the island by descendants of Jamaican Maroons (escaped slaves) in the 1700s.

Mesolectal forms are similar to very Basilectal Belizean Kriol.

Jamaican Patois exists mostly as a spoken language. Although standard British English is used for most writing in Jamaica, Jamaican Patois has been gaining ground as a literary language for almost a hundred years. Claude McKay published his book – written in Jamaican Patois – of Jamaican poems *Songs of Jamaica* in 1909 and 1912.

Patois and English are frequently used for stylistic contrast (code switching) in new forms of Internet writing.

Jamaican pronunciation and vocabulary are significantly different from Standard English despite heavy use of English words or derivatives.

A native speaker of a non-Caribbean English dialect can understand a heavily accented Jamaican speaker only if he/she speaks slowly and forgoes the use of the many idioms that are common in Jamaican.

Jamaican Patois displays similarities to the pidgin and creole languages of West Africa due to their common descent from the blending of African substrate languages with European languages.

Sociolinguistic variation

Jamaican Patois is a creole language that exhibits a gradation between more conservative creole forms and forms virtually identical to Standard English (i.e. metropolitan Standard English).

This situation came about with contact between speakers of a number of Niger-Congo languages and various dialects of English, the latter of which were all perceived as prestigious and the use of which carried socio-economic rewards.

The span of a speaker's command of the continuum generally corresponds to the variety of social situations that they situate themselves in.

Orthography

Because Jamaican Patois is a non-standard language, there is no standard or official way of writing it. For example, the word "there" can be written *de*, *deh*, or *dere*, and the word "three" is most commonly spelled *tree*, but it can be spelled *tri* or *trii* to distinguish it from the noun tree.

Often, Standard English spellings are used even when words are pronounced differently. Other times, a spelling has become widespread even though it is neither phonetic nor standard (eg. *pickney* = child). In this case the spelling *pikni* would be more phonetic).

However, due to increased use on the Internet (such as in E-mail) in recent years, a user-driven process of partial standardization has been taking place.

Vocabulary

Jamaican Patois contains many loan words. Primarily these come from English. But they are also borrowed from Spanish, Portuguese, Hindi, Arawak and African languages.

Examples from African languages include /dopi/ meaning ghost, from the Twi word *adope*; /se/ meaning *that* (in the sense of "he told me that...." = /im tel mi se/), also taken from Ashanti Twi; the pronoun /unu/, used for the plural form of you, is taken from the Igbo language.

Red eboe describes a light-skinned black person because of the reported account of fair skin among the Igbo.

Soso meaning *only* comes from both the Igbo and Yoruba languages.

From the Igbo language comes *Obeah*, a form of African shamanism (and also used as a popular scapegoat for common woes) originating from the Igbo *dibia* or *obia* ('doctoring') herbalists and spiritualists.

Words from Hindi include *nuh, ganja* (marijuana), and *janga* (crawdad).

Pickney or *pickiney* meaning child, taken from an earlier form (piccaninny) was ultimately borrowed from the Portuguese *pequenino* (the diminutive of *pequeno*, small) or Spanish *pequeño* ('small').

There are many words referring to popular produce and food items – *ackee, callaloo, guinep, bammy, roti, dal, kamranga.*

Jamaican Patois has its own rich variety of swearwords. One of the strongest is *blood claat* (along with related forms *raas claat*, *bomba claat*, *pussy claat* and others – compare with *bloody* in Australian English, which is not considered swearing). Homosexual men are referred to as /biips/ or *batty boys*.

Literature and film

A rich body of literature has developed in Jamaican Patois. Notable among early authors are Thomas MacDermot's *All Jamaica Library* and Claude McKay's *Songs of Jamaica* (1909), and, more recently, Linton Kwesi Johnson and Mikey Smith.

Subsequently, the life-work of Louise Bennett or Miss Lou (1919–2006), is particularly notable in her use of the rich colourful patois, despite being shunned by traditional literary groups. "The Jamaican Poetry League excluded her from its meetings, and editors failed to include her in anthologies." She argued forcefully for the recognition of Jamaican as a full language, with the same pedigree as the dialect from which Standard English had sprung:

Dah language weh yuh proud a,
Weh yuh honour an respec –

Po Mas Charlie, yuh no know se

Dat it spring from dialec!

—*Bans a Killin*

After the 1960s, the status of Jamaican rose as a number of respected linguistic studies were published, by Cassidy (1961,1967), Bailey (1966) and others.

Subsequently, it has gradually become mainstream to

codemix or write complete pieces in Jamaican Patois; proponents include Kamau Braithwaite who also analyses the position of Creole poetry in his *History of the Voice: The Development of Nation Language in Anglophone Caribbean Poetry* (1984).

However, Standard English remains the more prestigious literary medium in Jamaican literature.

Canadian-Caribbean science-fiction novelist Nalo Hopkinson often writes in Jamaican or other Caribbean patois.

Jamaican Patois is also presented in some films, for example, Tia Dalma's speech from Pirates of the Caribbean: Dead Man's Chest.

Emigration

Many Jamaicans have emigrated to other countries, especially to the United Kingdom, the United States, and to Canada. In the case of the United States, about 20,000 Jamaicans per year are granted permanent residence.

A very large number of them lived abroad where they collectively constitute what has become known as the Jamaican diaspora.

There has also been emigration of Jamaicans to Cuba. The scale of emigration has been widespread and similar to other Caribbean entities such as Puerto Rico, Guyana, and Trinidad and Tobago.

It's estimated that up to 2.5 million Jamaicans and Jamaican descendants live abroad. An estimated 60 per cent of the highly educated people of Jamaica now live abroad.

Concentrations of Jamaicans are large in a number of cities in the United States, including – in addition to the ones named earlier – Buffalo, Atlanta, Chicago, Orlando, Tampa, Philadelphia, Providence in Rhode Island, and Los Angeles.

Jamaicans in the United Kingdom number an estimated 800,000 making them by far the country's largest Afro-Caribbean group.

Large-scale migration from Jamaica to the UK occurred primarily in the 1950s and 1960s (when the country was still under British rule). Today, Jamaican communities exist in most large UK cities.

Jamaicans also live in Ireland and are mostly concentrated in nation's capital Dublin.

In Canada, the Jamaican population is centred in Toronto. And there are smaller communities in cities such as Hamilton, Montreal, Vancouver and Ottawa.

Jamaican diaspora

Jamaicans can be found in the far corners of the world but the largest pools of Jamaicans exist in the United States, the United Kingdom, Canada, other Caribbean islands, and all across the Caribbean coast of Central America.

During the past several decades, close to one million Jamaicans have emigrated especially to the United States, the United Kingdom and Canada. This emigration appears to have been tapering off somewhat in recent years.

Most Jamaican emigrants have followed a path first to the UK. Many who do not remain in the UK move on to other Commonwealth countries such as Canada.

Jamaican emigrants also migrate directly to the United States, Canada, other Caribbean nations, Central and South America – mainly Costa Rica and Brazil, and even Africa, most notably to Egypt and Ethiopia – for whatever reason since almost none of them originated from those two countries but are mostly of West African origin from what is now Nigeria, Ghana, Benin, Togo, Ivory Coast and other countries in that region.

New York City is home to a large Jamaican diaspora

community, with communities along Flatbush, Nostrand and Utica Avenues in Brooklyn – centred around the neighbourhoods of Prospect Heights, Lefferts Gardens, Flatbush, East Flatbush, Crown Heights, Canarsie, and Flatlands.

The Bronx, neighbourhoods and towns such as Wakefield, Eastchester, Baychester, Queens, Westchester county and nearby Stamford in Connecticut, also have significant Jamaican communities.

Flatbush, Nostrand, and Utica Avenues feature miles of Jamaican cuisine, food markets and other businesses, nightlife and residential enclaves.

In Toronto, the Jamaican community is also large. Caribbean areas of the city are located in the neighbourhoods of Rexdale in Etobicoke, Jane and Finch and Lawrence Heights in North York, Malvern in Scarborough, sections of downtown Toronto, and York, which also includes a Little Jamaica district that's identifiable along Eglinton Avenue West.

In recent years, many Jamaicans have been moving out to suburbs such as Mississauga and Brampton.

The Jamaican community also has had an influence on Toronto's culture. Caribana – the celebration of Caribbean culture – is an annual event in the city. The parade is held downtown on the first Saturday of August, shutting down a portion of Lake Shore Boulvevard.

Jamaica Day is in July, and the Jesus in the City parade attracts many Jamaican Christians. Reggae and dancehall are popular among Toronto's youth.

London in the United Kingdom has a strong Jamaican diaspora. An estimated 7% of Londoners are of Jamaican heritage. Many are now at least second-, if not third- or fourth-generation Black British Caribbeans.

Also a further 2% of people in London are of mixed Jamaican and British origin, the largest mixed-race group in the UK and the fastest-growing.

One of the largest and most famous Jamaican

communities is in Brixton, South London. More large Jamaican communities in London are Tottenham and Hackney in North London, Harlesden in North-West London, and Lewisham in South-East London.

The highest concentration of Jamaicans are in the inner-city South London boroughs.

On the last bank holiday of the year during late August, the Annual Notting Hill Carnival takes place in west London which is the second-biggest street party in the world after the Rio Carnival. It spans areas of west London such as Shepherd's Bush, Ladbroke Grove, White City and of course Notting Hill.

Many other Caribbean nations have large communities in that part of London. They include Trinidad and Tobago, Barbados, and Antigua and Barbuda.

The Caribbean community including many Jamaicans are involved in the carnival which starts on Saturday and finishes late on Monday.

Jamaicans have many food stalls, sound systems and floats involved in the procession.

More thanWell one million Londoners go to Notting Hill on the Monday for the carnival.

There is also a much smaller carnival called the Tottenham Carnival which takes place in Tottenham in June every year. Approximately 40,000 people attend the carnival.

Other Jamaican communities in the UK are in St. Pauls in Bristol, Chapeltown in Leeds, Moss Side, Longsight and Hulme in Manchester, Toxteth in Liverpool, Burngreave in Sheffield, Handsworth, Lozells, and Aston in Birmingham, and St. Ann's, Nottingham.

More recently many resort and wild-life management skilled Jamaicans have been trending emigration toward such far-flung nations as Australia, New Zealand, the Philippines, Malaysia and Indonesia.

Jamaica continues to have a severe problem with barrel children – those left on their own by parents seeking a better life abroad.

Crime

Jamaica has had one of the highest murder rates in the world for many years, according to UN estimates.

Former Prime Minister P. J. Patterson described the situation as "a national challenge of unprecedented proportions."

In 2005, Jamaica had 1,674 murders for a murder rate of 58 per 100,000 people. The island nation had the highest murder rate in the world during that year.

In November 2008, the Jamaican parliament voted to retain the death penalty which is performed by hanging.

Some areas of Jamaica, particularly cities such as Kingston, experience high levels of crime and violence.

There is also violence against homosexuals. The U.S. Department of State reported that brutality against homosexuals, mainly by private citizens, was widespread in 2008.

Homosexuality is illegal in Jamaica, incurring a prison sentence. Many Jamaicans are hostile towards LGBT (lesbian, gay, bisexual, and trans-gender) and inter-sex people, and various mob attacks against gay people have been reported.

Some critics claim that attacks on gay people are encouraged in some popular Jamaican dancehall/reggae songs that are sometimes referred to as murder music.

Attacks on gays has been criticised by human rights groups which have described Jamaica as "the most homophobic place on earth."

Religion

By far the largest religion in Jamaica is the Christian faith. The Anglican Church, and the Church of God are throughout the country, and many old churches have been carefully maintained and/or restored.

The Rastafarian religion is a folk derivative of the larger Christian culture, likely influenced by Ethiopian Coptic culture.

There are also a small number of Jewish synagogues in Jamaica, dating from 17th century.

Elements of ancient African religions remain in remote areas through out the island. Most of the practices are described as Obeah, Kumina, or Pocomania. Although the congregations of these traditional "churches" are small, they are visited by many Christian and non Christians seeking traditional solutions which can not be found in conventional churches or other religious organisations.

It's estimated that as much as 80% of the population secretly seek the services of the African traditional religious healers when confronted with serious problems that conventional medicine and society can not remedy.

According to the 2001 census, the country's largest denominations are the Church of God (24% of the country's total population); Seventh-day Adventist (SDA) Church (11%); Pentecostal (10%); Baptist (7%); Anglican (4%); Roman Catholic (2%); United Church (2%); Methodist (2%); Jehovah's Witnesses (2%); Moravian (1%); and Plymouth Brethren (1%).

The Christian faith gained credibility as British Christian abolitionists and Baptist missionaries joined educated former slaves in the campaign against slavery.

The Rastafari movement had 24,020 adherents in Jamaica in 2001, according to census figures. But there are some disputes on this number. There are those who claim there are far more Rastas in Jamaica than what the government says.

The Rastafari movement is a monotheistic, Abrahamic, new religious organisation which was started in Jamaica in the 1930s. Its adherents worship Emperor Haile Selassie of Ethiopia and they don't believe that he died because he is

God incarnate. Therefore he could not have died because God does not die. They see him as representing the Second Advent. The followers of this religion are known as Rastafarians, or Rastas.

The movement is sometimes referred to as "Rastafarianism" but the term is considered to be derogatory and offensive by some Rastas who dislike their faith being labelled as an "ism."

Rastafari is not a highly organised religion; it's a movement and an ideology.

Many Rastas say it's not a "religion" at all but a "way of life."

Most Rastas don't claim membership in any religious sect or denomination and encourage one another to find faith and inspiration within themselves; although some of them do identify strongly with one of the "mansions of Rastafari" – the three most prominent of these being the *Nyahbinghi*, the *Bobo Ashanti* and the *Twelve Tribes of Israel*.

The name *Rastafari* is taken from *Ras Tafari*, the pre-regnal title of Haile Selassie I, composed of the word *Ras* which in the Amharic language literally means "Head," an Ethiopian title equivalent to the English title "Duke," and Haile Selassie's pre-regnal given name, Tafari.

Rastafari are generally distinguished for asserting the doctrine that Haile Selassie I, the former, and final, Emperor of Ethiopia, is another incarnation of the Christian God called Jah. They see Haile Selassie I as *Jah* or *Jah Rastafari*, who is the second coming of Jesus Christ onto the Earth.

The Rastafari movement encompasses themes such as the spiritual use of cannabis and the rejection of Western society which they call Babylon in reference more to the metaphoric Babylon of Christianity than to the historical Mesopotamian city which is also mentioned in the Bible.

It proclaims Africa – which is also called Zion in the lexicon of Rastafarians – as the original birthplace of mankind, and embraces various Afrocentric social and political doctrines and aspirations including the social and political views and teachings of Jamaican black nationalist Marcus Garvey who is also often regarded as a prophet by Rastas. Marcus Garvey led the "back to Africa" movement.

Today, awareness of the Rastafari movement has spread in many parts of the world, largely through interest generated by reggae music. The most notable examples of Rasta-men are Bob Marley and Peter Tosh, who were both singers and songwriters with an international reputation as reggae musicians. Bob Marley died in 1981, and Peter Tosh in 1988.

By 1997, there were about one million Rastafarians worldwide, including some in Africa. About 5 – 10% of Jamaicans identify themselves as Rastafarians.

Other religions in Jamaica include the Bahá'í Faith which counts perhaps 8,000 adherents and 21 Local Spiritual Assemblies; Islam, Buddhism, and Hinduism.

There is also a small population of Jews, about 200, who describe themselves as Liberal-Conservative. The first Jews in Jamaica trace their roots back to early 15th century Spain and Portugal.

Muslim groups in Jamaica claim 5,000 adherents.

Culture

Jamaican culture represents a rich blend of cultures. The indigenous people – Amerindians known as Taino – followed by their Spanish conquerors who were in turn conquered by the British, have all made major contributions to Jamaican culture.

However, it's the blacks and slaves who became the dominant cultural force as they suffered and resisted the harsh conditions of forced labour. Their culture was African adapted to Jamaica's local conditions.

After the abolition of slavery, Chinese and Indian migrants transported to the island as indentured workers, brought their cultures from Asia.

Although Jamaica is a small nation, it has been a major cultural force through the years and has had a global impact mainly because of its internationally acclaimed reggae music.

The musical genres of reggae, ska, mento, rocksteady, dub and, more recently, dancehall and ragga originated in the island's vibrant, popular urban recording industry.

Jamaica also played an important role in the development of punk rock through reggae and ska.

Reggae has also influenced American rap music, since they both share their roots as rhythmic, African styles of music. Like reggae, rap music has strong African elements in terms of style and performance but not always in terms of lyrics many of which are culturally offensive to Africans; for example, the use of profanity and insults to women so common among rap artists and their lyrics.

Some rappers such as The Notorious B.I.G. And Heavy D are of Jamaican descent.

Many other internationally known artists are Jamaicans or were born in Jamaica. They include Jimmy Cliff, Bunny Wailer, Grace Jones, Lee "Scratch" Perry, Desmond Dekker, Dennis Brown, Joseph Hill, Big Youth, Beres Hammond, Beenie Man, Shaggy, Shabba Ranks, Super Cat, Buju Banton, Sean Paul, I Wayne, Bounty Killer and many others.

Famous band artist groups that came from Jamaica include Culture, Black Uhuru, Third World Band, Inner Circle, Chalice Reggae Band, Fab Five, and Morgan Heritage.

The genre jungle emerged from London's Jamaican diaspora.

The birth of hip-hop in New York City also owed much to the city's Jamaican community.

The Rastafari movement has also been a major cultural

force in Jamaica through the years especially since the 1930s. This Back to Africa movement believes that Haile Selassie is a black messiah who came to take the lost Twelve Tribes of Israel back to live with him on Holy Mount Zion in a world of perfect peace, love and harmony.

Bob Marley was the most prominent convert to the Rastafari faith. He spread the message of Rastafari to the world as did Peter Tosh, another international luminary, and others who are still doing it today.

Peter Tosh was also the driving force behind the formation of the reggae music group, The Wailers, whose members were Peter Tosh himself, Bob Marley and Bunny Wailer. Peter Tosh was the only one among the three who knew how to play guitar and other instruments when they founded the group. And it was he who taught Bob Marley how to play guitar.

The practice of smoking marijuana throughout Jamaica was popularised as a direct result of the Rastafarians' use of this weed for meditation purposes. And the popularity of the Rastafarian movement out of Jamaica through music helped increase the use of cannabis worldwide as it was promoted as "the weed of wisdom."

Jamaica has also been featured prominently in literature and films. For example, Ian Fleming who lived in Jamaica repeatedly used the island as a setting for the James Bond novels, including *Live and Let Die, Doctor No, For Your Eyes Only, The Man with the Golden Gun,* and *Octopussy.*

But the only James Bond film adaption to have been set in Jamaica, so far, is *Doctor No*. Filming for the fictional island of San Monique in *Live and Let Die*, however, took place in Jamaica.

Journalist and author H. G. de Lisser (1878–1944) who was Jamaican used his native country as the setting for his many novels.

Born at Falmouth, de Lisser worked as a reporter for

the *Jamaica Times* at a young age and in 1920 began publishing the magazine *Planters' Punch*. *The White Witch of Rosehall* is one of his better known novels.

He was named Honorary President of the Jamaican Press Association and worked throughout his professional career to promote the Jamaican sugar industry.

The American film *Cocktail* starring Tom Cruise is one of the most popular films to depict Jamaica.

A look at delinquent youth in Jamaica is presented in the 1970s musical crime film *The Harder They Come* starring Jimmy Cliff as a frustrated – and psychopathic – reggae musician who descends into a murderous crime spree.

Another popular Jamaican-based film is the 1993 comedy *Cool Runnings* which is loosely based on the true story of Jamaica's first bobsled team trying to make it in the Winter Olympics.

Errol Flynn lived with his third wife Patrice Wymore in Port Antonio in the 1950s. He was responsible for developing tourism to that area, popularising raft trips down rivers on bamboo rafts.

The island is also famous for its Jamaican jerk spice which forms a popular part of Jamaican cuisine.

Jamaica is also home to the world-renowned Red Stripe beer and Jamaican Blue Mountain Coffee.

Rastafari: A closer look

One of the most prominent and internationally known aspects of Jamaica's African-Caribbean culture is the Rastafari movement, particularly those elements that are expressed through reggae music.

In the 1970s and early 1980s, Robert Nesta Marley – Bob Marley – became the most high-profile exponent of the Rastafari culture and beliefs. His reputation as an innovative musician devoted to his faith has continued to grow since his death. By 2004, his "greatest hits" compilation, "Legend," had sold 20 million copies worldwide, making him arguably the world's most famous Jamaican and certainly Jamaica's biggest-selling recording artist.

Rastafari itself, a monotheistic belief system, is based on teachings found in the Old Testament and the New Testament, especially the Book of Revelations. However, what distinguishes Rastafari from Christianity, Islam and Judaism – all of which also cite Abrahamic beliefs and teachings – is that Rastas believe in the divinity of Emperor Haile Selassie of Ethiopia.

Hailed by Rastas as H.I.M – His Imperial Majesty – Haile Selassie is regarded as the true descendant of King Solomon and the earthly embodiment of Jah (God) – what believers see as a fulfillment of prophesy regarding the second coming of the Messiah.

It should be noted that those Rasta beliefs which are not explicitly mentioned in the Bible – such as the specific name of H.I.M. 'Haile Selassie' – have not been compiled as a single holy text. Instead, Rasta beliefs are primarily shared through a community of songs, chants and oral testimonies, as well as in written texts. The extensive use of songs makes Rastafari a particularly musical source of Jamaican culture.

Rasta cultural traditions include wearing their hair in uncut, uncombed strands known as dreadlocks in adherence to the Nazarite vow, as well as eating unprocessed – natural – foodstuffs which are known as *Ital*. However, neither tradition is regarded as compulsory. Many people who wear dreadlocks are not Rastas. And many Rastas do not wear dreadlocks.

One of the most controversial cultural traditions is Rastas' use of *ganja* as a sacrament which is smoked to aid in reasoning – contemplation and discussion. Cannabis is a strictly prohibited substance in Jamaica. Therefore its use by Rastas means the movement is in a more-or-less permanent state of tension with police agencies.

In its Jamaican homeland, Rastafari is a minority culture and receives little official recognition. But it's a prominent feature of Jamaican identity even if it's not the dominant one.

Jamaica is an overwhelmingly Christian country. Therefore Rasta beliefs and practices – such as the divinity of H.I.M Haile Selassie – are sometimes regarded not only as unorthodox but pagan by Christian Jamaicans although some Rastas can also express hostility towards some aspects of Christianity.

Nevertheless, the artistic contributions of the movement, especially by Bob Marley and Peter Tosh, are widely respected. Bob Marley was awarded the Jamaican Order of Merit in 1981 and there are two official monuments to him

Rastas can be found in many countries outside Jamaica and among many non-Jamaicans. Because it's not a centrally organised religion, there is no way of knowing how many devotees there are.

Dance

Dance has always been important in Jamaica – from colonial times until the present. It's an integral part of national life and culture.

Early folk rhythms and movements often enhanced Christian religious celebrations or were associated with Christian holidays. More recently, dances have been associated with the music of Jamaica, particularly dancehall styles.

More than 30 distinctive Jamaican dances have been identified. According to the National Library of Jamaica, traditional Jamaican dances fall roughly under three categories: African-derived, European-derived and Creole.

The African-derived dance tradition is divided into two

types: religious dances and social dances.

Religious African dances such as the ritualistic Kumina, Myal, and Pocomania, are integral parts of worship ceremonies. The aim is to bring the dancers into the realm of the spiritual and heighten their readiness for possession. This part of Jamaica's African heritage has mainly been preserved by the Maroon communities.

Social African-derived dances include Etu Quadrille.

The Jamaican Creole dances integrate elements from both European and African cultures. Examples are Maypole, originally religious but now mainly social; Jonkonnu; Bruckin's; Revival; Pukkumina, possibly the best-known Revival – religious – style which still exists today; and Dinkie mini, a dance in the Wake Complex of traditional dances.

Social dances that are European-derived include those which accompanied work songs and ring games.

Dance is also represented during the Jamaican Hosay, a Caribbean East Indian festival.

Jonkonnu and Hosay are considered secular dances, despite the performance of Jonkonnu around Christmas time.

Dance theatre is also growing in importance. Rex Nettleford, Eddy Thomas, Olive Lewin, and Edna Marley are four Jamaicans whose influences on the arts – music and dance in particular – has been extremely important. Nettleford, Thomas, and Ivy Baxter formed the National Dance Theatre Company in the 1950s.

Other important Jamaicans in dance theatre have included the Tony-Award-winning choreographer Garth Fagan (*The Lion King* on Broadway).

Dancehall, or ragga music has inspired a number of dance styles as well.

To understand the evolution of popular dance, it helps to understand the musical progression.

Ska music, with fast beats, also had fast dances.

The slow to rocksteady also developed slower dances,

allowing dancers to stay on the floor longer.

Reggae is associated with many things including the Rastafarian movement but it also influenced the newer styles.

Dancehall music often creates its own dances based on moves in the lyrics of the songs themselves.

Soca music from Trinidad and Tobago is popular in Jamaica with most of the popular artists being from Trinidad. But there are many soca Jamaican artists such as Byron Lee, Fab 5, and Lovindeer who are also famous and represent Jamaican music.

Music of Jamaica

The music of Jamaica includes Jamaican folk music and many popular genres such as mento, ska, rocksteady, reggae, dub music, dancehall, reggae fusion and related styles.

Jamaica's music culture is a fusion of elements from the United States – rhythm and blues (R&B), rock and roll, soul, jazz and other styles; also elements from Africa, and neighbouring Caribbean islands such as Trinidad and Tobago whose music, calypso and soca, has influenced Jamaican music in varying degrees.

Reggae is especially popular mainly because of Bob Marley's international fame. He's called the king of reggae.

Jamaican music's influence on music styles in other countries includes the practice of toasting which has had an impact on rap music in the United States.

British genres such as Lovers rock and jungle music have also been influenced by Jamaican music.

Mentos

Mento was recorded in Jamaica in the 1950s because of the efforts of Stanley Motta who noted the similarities between Jamaican folk and Trinidadian calypso which was becoming popular around the world.

For decades, mento bands toured the big hotels in Jamaica.

While mento never found as large an international audience as calypso, some mento recordings by Count Lasher, Lord Composer and George Moxey, among others, are now widely-respected legends of Jamaican music. Today, mento has largely been supplanted by other forms of music such as reggae and dub. But it's still performed, recorded, and released internationally by traditionalist performers like the Jolly Boys.

Jazz

From the early 1900s and through the years, Jamaica has produced many notable jazz musicians. The Alpha School in Kingston which provided training and encouragement in music education was very influential. Also significant was the brass band tradition of the island, strengthened by opportunities for musical work and training in military contexts.

However, limited scope for a career in jazz music in Jamaica resulted in many local jazz musicians leaving the island. Many of them left Jamaica and went to live and work in the United Kingdom, especially London, or in the United States.

Among the most prominent and influential Jamaican jazz instrumentalists who made successful careers abroad was alto saxophonist Joe Harriot who is considered to be one of the most original and most innovative jazz composers in history.

Also internationally successful were trumpeters Dizzy Reece, Leslie 'Jiver' Hutchinson and Leslie Thompson.; bassist Coleridge Goode; guitarist Ernest Ranglin; and pianist Monty Alexander.

Harriott, Goode, Hutchinson and Thompson built their

careers in London, along with many other instrumentalists such as pianist Yorke de Souza and the outstanding saxophonist Bertie King who later returned to Jamaica and formed a mento-style band.

Reece and Alexander worked in the United States. Saxophonist Wilton 'Bogey' Gaynair settled in Germany working mainly with Kurt Edelhagen's orchestra.

Ska

Ska originated in Jamaica in the late 1950s. Some of the first songs identified as ska were "Manny-O" by Joe Higgs (1958), "Easy Snapping" by Theophilus Beckford (1959), and "Oh! Carolina" by the Folkes Brothers (1960). "Simmer Down," a huge ska hit, was recorded by The Wailers in 1963.

Perhaps the best-known of the original ska bands were The Skatalites whose career spanned decades and transcended Jamaican musical genres. The Skatalites' music launched the careers of Tommy McCook, virtuoso trombonist Don Drummond and tenor saxophonist, and fellow Alpha Boys School graduates Roland Alphonso, Jackie Mittoo, and Lester Sterling.

At first primarily instrumental, ska's rhythms generally didn't lend well to vocal stylings. However, some popular singers such as Desmond Decker, Toots Hibbert and Bob Marley got their start by singing in this style. This new style was widely embraced by Jamaican youths, and soon became popular in the United Kingdom and around the world.

In 1963, Chris Blackwell brought teenage singer Millie Small to Great Britain. She exploded on the international scene with her hit, "My Boy Lollipop," which climbed the charts to Number 2 in both Great Britain and the United States.

Live touring bands launched the careers of many ska, rocksteady and reggae artists. Tommy McCook had been part of the band of Aubrey Adams based at the Courtleigh Manor hotel in Kingston before becoming one of the founding members of the Skatalites. Drummer Lloyd Knibb, also of The Skatalites, had done the hotel circuit playing for the Val Bennett, Len Hibbert and Cecil Lloyd bands.

One of the most successful music groups in Jamaica was Billy Vernon and the Celestials, the resident band at the Yellow Bird Club in Montego Bay. They toured many of the island's leading hotels. Their work was a blend of ska, mento and jump up, and featured hits such as "Ska Suzanna," "Yellow Bird" and Wings of A Dove."

A number of artists including Errol "E.T." Webster, also known as "Errol T," got their start in the music business with Billy Vernon and the Celestials.

Chris Blackwell's Island Records became the biggest label promoting Jamaican music on the international market. Due to its affiliation with the record industry in the UK and good financial support – especially the United Kingdom and the United States – Island Records had the distribution capacity to vastly increase exposure of Jamaican music to the global pop market, especially in the UK where a significant population of Jamaicans had relocated.

Ska's popularity grew steadily in Jamaica alongside Rastafari which spread rapidly in impoverished urban areas and among the politically radical musicians.

The lyrics of ska songs began to focus on Rastafarian themes; slower beats and chants entered the music from religious Rastafarian music, and ska soon evolved into rocksteady.

Rocksteady

Rocksteady was the music of Jamaica's rude boys by the mid-1960s when The Wailers and The Clarendonians dominated the charts, taking over from pioneers like Alton

Ellise who is believed to have invented rocksteady.

Desmond Dekker's "007" brought international attention to the new genre.

The mix put heavy emphasis on the bass line as opposed to ska's strong horn section; and the rhythm guitar began playing on the upbeat.

Session musicians such as Supersonics, Soul Vendors, Jets and Jackie Mittoo of the Skatalites, became popular during that period.

Reggae

By the early 1970s, rocksteady had evolved into reggae which combines elements from American soul music with the traditional shuffle and one-drop of Jamaican mento.

Reggae quickly became popular around the world due in large part to the international success of Bob Marley, Peter Tosh, Bunny Wailer and other reggae musicians.

Bob Marley was viewed as a Rastafarian messianic figure by some fans especially in the Caribbean, and in Africa, as well as among some Native Americans and Australian Aborigines.

His lyrics about love, redemption and natural beauty captivated audiences and he gained headlines for negotiating truces between the two opposing Jamaican political parties (at the One Love Concert), led by Michael Manley (PNP) and Edward Seaga (JLP).

Reggae music was intricately tied to the expansion of the Rastafarian religion and its principles of pacifism and pan-Africanism. Musicians such as Gregory Isaacs, The Congos, and Burning Spear and producers like Lee 'Scratch" Perry solidified the early sound of reggae.

Dub

By 1973, dub music had emerged as a distinct reggae genre and heralded the dawn of the remix. .

Developed by record producers such as Lee "Scratch" Perry and King Tubby, dub featured previously-recorded songs remixed with prominence on the bass. Often the lead instruments and vocals would drop in and out of the mix, sometimes processed heavily with studio effects.

King Tubby's advantage came from his intimate knowledge with audio gear and his ability to build his own sound systems and recording studios that were superior to the competition. He became famous for his remixes of recordings made by others as well as those he recorded in his own studio.

Following in Tubby's footsteps came artists such as U-Roy and Big Youth who used Rasta chants in songs.

Until the end of the 1970s, Big Youth-inspired dub music with chanted vocals dominated Jamaican popular music.

At the very end of the decade, dancehall artists like Ranking Joe, Lone Ranger and General Echo brought a return to U-Roy's style.

Dancehall and ragga

During the 1980s, the most popular music styles in Jamaica were dancehall and ragga.

Dancehall is essentially speechfying with musical accompaniment including a basic drum beat most often played on electric drums.

The lyrics moved away from the political and spiritual lyrics popular in the 1970s and now concentrate more on less serious issues.

Ragga is characterised by the use of computerized beats and sequenced melodic tracks. It's usually said to have been invented with the song "Under Mi Sleng Teng" by Wayne Smith.

Ragga barely edged out dancehall as the dominant form of Jamaican music in the 1980s. DJ Shabba Ranks and vocalist team Chaka Demus and Pliers proved more enduring than the competition and helped inspire an updated version of the rude boy culture called raggamuffin.

Dancehall was sometimes violent in lyrical content and several rival performers made headlines with their feuds across Jamaica, most notably Beenie Man versus Bounty Killer.

It emerged from pioneering recordings in the late 1970s by Barrington Levy, with Roots Radics backing and Junjo Lawes as producer.

The Roots Radics were the pre-eminent backing band for the dancehall style. Yellowman, Ini Kamoze, Charlie Chaplin and General Echo helped popularise the style along with producers like Sugar Minott.

The 1980s saw a rise in reggae music outside Jamaica. During that period, reggae particularly influenced African popular music: Sonny Okusuns (Nigeria), John Chibadura (Zimbabwe), Lucky Dube (South Africa) and Alpha Blondy (Ivory Coast) became stars.

The 1980s saw the end of the dub era in Jamaica, although dub has remained a popular and influential style in the UK and to a lesser extent throughout Europe and the United States.

Dub in the 1990s merged with electronic music.

Variations of dancehall continued to be popular into the mid 1990s. Some of the performers of the previous decade converted to Rastafari and changed their lyrical content. Artists like Buju Banton experienced significant crossover success in foreign markets, while Beenie Man, Bounty Killer and others developed a sizable North American following due to their frequent guest spots on albums by gangsta rappers such as Wu-Tang Clan and Jay-Z..

Some ragga musicians including Beenie Man, Shabba Ranks and Capleton adopted a new style of lyrics.

Reggae fusion

Reggae fusion emerged as a popular sub-genre in the late 1990s.

It's a mixture of reggae or dancehall with elements of other genres such as hip hop, rhythm and blues (R&B), jazz, rock 'n roll or indie rock. It's closely related to ragga music.

Non-Rastafarian Jamaican religious music

The Bongo Nation is a distinct group of Jamaicans possibly descended from the Congo. They are known for Kumina which refers to both a religion and a form of music.

Kumina's distinctive drumming style became one of the roots of Rastafarian drumming, itself the source of the distinctive Jamaican rhythm heard in ska, rocksteady and reggae.

The modern intertwining of Jamaican religion and music can be traced back to the 1860s when the Pocomania and Revival Zion churches drew on African traditions and incorporated music into almost every facet of worship. Later, this trend spread into Hindu communities, resulting in baccra music.

The spread of Rastafari into urban Jamaica in the 1960s transformed the Jamaican music scene which incorporated drumming (played at grounation ceremonies) and which has led to today's popular music.

Many of the above mentioned music and dance have been stylised by the National Dance Theatre Company of Jamaica led by Prof. Rex Nettleford artistic director (ret, prof and vice chancellor of The University of the West Indies) and Marjorie Whyle Musical Director (Caribbean Musicologist, pianist, drummer, arranger lecturer at the

University of the West Indies).

Since 1962, this volunteer company of dancers and musicians have had many of these dances in its core repertoire and have performed worldwide to large audiences including The British Royal family.

Jamaican cuisine

History

Cuisine of the Tainos

Christopher Columbus visited Jamaica several times towards the end of the 1400s and at the beginning of the 1500s. He was once even shipwrecked off the northern coast of the island for about two years from 1503 to 1504.

During these visits, he described the way the Arawaks – the indigenous inhabitants of Jamaica – preserved meat by adding peppers, allspice and sea salt to make what is now known as Jamaican jerk spice.

The cuisine of Jamaica includes a mixture of cooking techniques, flavours, spices and influences from the indigenous people on the island, Spanish and British settlers, African slaves, Indians and Chinese who collectively constitute the island's multi-ethnic and multiracial society.

It's also influenced by the crops introduced into the island from tropical southeast Asia.

Jamaican cuisine includes various dishes from the different cultures brought to the island. Other dishes are novel or a fusion of techniques and traditions. In addition to ingredients that are native to Jamaica, many foods have been introduced and are now grown locally. A wide variety of seafood, tropical fruits and meats are available.

Some Jamaican cuisine dishes are variations of the cuisines and cooking styles brought to the island from different parts of the world. These are often modified to incorporate local products. Others are novel and have been developed locally.

Popular Jamaican dishes include curry goat, fried dumplings, ackee and salt fish, fried plantain, "jerk," steamed cabbage and "rice and peas" – pigeon peas or kidney beans.

Jamaican and various pastries and breads as well as fruit beverages and Jamaican rum are also popular.

Jamaican cuisine has spread with emigrations, especially during the 20th century, from the island to other countries. This has been facilitated by the quest for better opportunities in different parts of the world.

Jamaican literature

Jamaica has been the home or birthplace of many important authors. One of the most important aspects of Jamaican literature is the local patois or creole.

Folk beginnings

The tradition of storytelling in Jamaica is a long one, beginning with folktales told by African slaves during the colonial era.

Jamaica's folk stories are closely associated with those of the Ashanti, the Igbo, the Yoruba, the Ewe and other African ethnic groups from which the slaves were taken.

Some European tales were also brought to the island, particularly those from the United Kingdom since Jamaica was a British possession.

In folktales, the local speech style is particularly necessary. It infuses humour into the stories and is an integral part of the story telling.

Perhaps the most popular character in Jamaican tales is Anancy; the African spelling is Anansi.

This is an African spider-god who makes an appearance in tales throughout the Caribbean.

He is a trickster god and often goes against other animal-god characters, like Tiger and Donkey, in his stories.

The character is also known as Nancy Spida, and Brer Nansi.

The stories were also used by the slaves to outsmart their masters.

Literature

Thomas MacDermot, a Jamaican, is credited for fostering the creation of Jamaican literature. And his work, *Becka's Buckra Baby*, is seen as the beginning of modern Caribbean literature.

Jamaican Claude McKay was one of the founding fathers of Harlem Renaissance. He was also one of the people who helped fuel Negritude.

Aime Cesaire of Martinique is seen by many people as the father of Negritude, a concept that was also forcefully articulated by the African poet and philosopher Leopold Sedar Senghor who for many years was also the president of Senegal.

Having established himself as a poet in Jamaica, McKay moved to the United States in his 20s. He later went to France. But he never returned to Jamaica.

Another well-known Jamaican poet is Una Marson. She was well-known for her poetry and her activism as a feminist. Yet another one is Louise Bennett-Coverly.

One internationally renowned author who is not Jamaican but who has ties to Jamaica is Derek Walcott, a Nobel laureate, from St Lucia. He studied at the University of the West Indies in Jamaica.

Other writers who have recently gained acclaim in Jamaica include Hazel Dorothy Campbell and the late Mikey Smith.

The island's local dialect, Jamaican Patois, has become an important element in literature and other arts. The speech style is particularly notable in poetry and in prose's dialogue.

Economy

Jamaica has a number of natural resources, especially bauxite, and a climate conducive to agriculture and tourism.

The discovery of bauxite in the 1940s and subsequent establishment of the bauxite-alumina industry changed Jamaica's economy. Before then, the emphasis was on the production of agricultural commodities as a means to fuel economic growth.

All that shifted to the production of bauxite and aluminium. By the 1970s, Jamaica had emerged as one of the world's leading producers of these minerals, leading to an increase in foreign investment in the country.

Jamaica has a mixed economy. State enterprises and private-sector businesses are both an integral part of the economy.

Major sectors of the Jamaican economy include agriculture, mining, manufacturing, tourism, financial and insurance services.

Tourism and mining are the leading earners of foreign exchange.

An estimated 1.3 million tourists visit Jamaica every year. Tourism is the largest foreign-exchange earner.

Jamaica is the second-largest exporter of bauxite in the world, surpassed only by Australia.

Primary industries

Agriculture

Sugar, the leading export crop, is produced in nearly every parish. It's also used for the production of by-products such as molasses and rum. Some wallboard is made from bagasse.

Bananas are another major export.

Another major export is coffee. It's grown mainly around the Blue Mountains and other hilly areas. It's a brand product known as Jamaican Blue Mountain Coffee which is considered to be among the best in the world.

The picking season for coffee lasts from August to March.

Another important crop is cocoa. It's grown throughout Jamaica. About a third of the cocoa is used within Jamaica for instant drinks and confectionery.

Citrus fruit is mainly grown in the central parts of Jamaica, particularly between the elevations of 1,000 – 2,500 feet. The fruit picking season lasts from November to April.

Two factories in May Pen and Bog Walk produce fruit juices, canned fruit, essential oils and marmalade.

Coconuts are grown in the coastal areas of the northern and eastern parts of the island. They provide enough copra to supply factories to make butterine, margarine, lard, edible oil and laundry soap.

Rice is grown in swampy areas around the Black River and around Long Bay in Hanover and Westmoreland parishes for local consumption.

Other export crops are pimento, ginger, tobacco, and sisal.

Animal husbandry

Pastures cover a significant part of the land in Jamaica. Cattle rearing is one of the important economic activities on the island.

There is an increase in the quantity of animal products and in the number of livestock. But they're not enough for local requirements.

Also, the production of dairy products has been significant through the years, partly fuelled by the existence of a condensed milk factory at Bog Walk which was built in 1940. Still, the supply of dairy products is not enough for local consumption and Jamaica imports large quantities of powdered milk, butter and cheese.

Fishing

The fishing industry grew during the 1980s mainly because of an increase in inland fishing on the island.

Thousands of people make a living from fishing. Many fishermen live on the Pedro Cays which are 80 miles off Jamaica's southern coast within the nation's territorial waters.

The shallow waters and cays off the southern coast of Jamaica have more fish than the northern part does.

Jamaica is able to meet about half of its fish requirements. The rest is imported. Major imports of frozen and salted fish come from the United States and Canada.

But some of the fish are toxic. Catfish are responsible for many deaths because of the deadly venom found on the tips of their dorsal and pectoral fins.

However, the deadly fish are considered by some people to be a delicacy.

Forestry

By the late 1980s, only 185,000 hectares (457,000 acres) of Jamaica's original 1,000,000 hectares (2,500,000 acres) of forest remained.

The forests that once covered Jamaica now exist only in mountainous areas. And they provide only 20% of the island's timber requirements.

The remaining forest is protected from further exploitation.

Other accessible mountain areas are being reforested mainly with pines, mahoe and mahogany.

Mining

Jamaica is one of the major producers of bauxite and alumina in the world.

The island has reserves of more than 2 billion tonnes of bauxite which are expected to last for 100 years.

The mineral is found in the central parishes of St. Elizabeth, Manchester, Clarendon, St. Catherine, St. Ann & Trelawny.

There are 4 alumina plants and 6 mines.

The island nation also has deposits of several million tonnes of gypsum on the southern slopes of the Blue Mountains.

A large amount of the mineral is used in the local cement industry and in the production of other building materials.

Other minerals found in Jamaica include marble, limestone, silica, copper, lead, zinc, manganese, and iron. Some of these minerals are found only in small quantities.

No oil deposits have been found.

Secondary Industries

The manufacturing sector is an important part of Jamaica's economy. It includes food processing; oil refining; production of chemicals; construction materials; plastic goods; paints; pharmaceuticals; cartons; leather goods; cigars; alcoholic drinks such as rum and beer; beverages; assembled electronics; textiles, and apparel.

The garment industry also is a major employer providing thousands of jobs.

An oil refinery located near Kingston refines crude oil imported from Venezuela. It also produces a number of petroleum by-products. These are mainly for local use.

There is significant growth in the construction industry because of the new hotels and tourist facilities which are being built to attract tourists to the island.

Tertiary industries

Tourism

Tourism, the island's main foreign exchange earner, provides about one-fourth of all the jobs in Jamaica.

Most of the tourist activity is centred on the island's northern coast including the areas of Montego Bay, Ocho Rios, and Port Antonio, as well as Negril on the island's western tip.

Financial services

The financial services industry has expanded rapidly through the years. It includes banking, investment, and insurance services.

Banks include Century National Bank, National Commercial Bank, Pan-Caribbean Bank, Scotia Bank,

Royal Bank of Canada, and First Global Bank.

Retail

Jamaica does not have large commercial centres besides Kingston, Montego Bay, and Ocho Rios. As a result of that, the island nation has a poorly developed retail sector.

While Kingston and Montego Bay are home to a number of retail stores including American fast-food franchises such as Domino's, Pizza Hut, and Dairy Queen, the majority of the towns in the interior – Mandeville, May Pen, Spanish Town and others – have only small shops, public markets, and temporary roadside stands.

The island of Jamaica has a high profile on the international scene. One of the reasons is that it's part of the Caribbean which is a major tourist destination.

The Caribbean islands have been immortalised in many ways. They have been glorified as "paradise." Songs have been written about them. They're also glorified in movies as the place to be under the sun.

And they may indeed be tropical paradise, with Jamaica being the most prominent island. But with all its prominence and attractions, Jamaica remains essentially a Third World country. Yet it has a lot of potential across the spectrum which has not been fully harnessed.

Conclusion

THIS work is intended to be a general introduction to the Caribbean. It's not intended to be an academic work, although some people may find it to be useful in that area as well.

When I started working on the project, I did not intend to compile academic material on the Caribbean. I simply wanted to gather some information – already available in the public domain – which would help some people to learn some basic facts about the islands covered in this work.

I hope I have achieved my goal.

The material is compiled in three volumes:

Caribbean Islands: The Land and The People
A Look at the Caribbean and Its People and Culture
Life in The Caribbean.

Lightning Source UK Ltd.
Milton Keynes UK
UKOW04f2036031013

218459UK00001B/201/P